Chart No.

United States of America

Nautical Chart Symbols Abbreviations and Terms

Tenth Edition
November 2000

Reprinted 2004

Published by:
Lighthouse Press^SM

a div. of *ProStar Publications, Inc.*^SM
3 Church Circle, Suite 109, Annapolis, MD 21401
(800) 481-6277   Fax (800) 487-6277

Email: editor@prostarpublications.com
www.prostarpublications.com

This publication contains data and associated information produced and obtained from the National Imagery and Mapping Agency (NIMA) and the Department of Commerce, NOAA, National Ocean Service. This title is published by a private company and any appearance of NIMA's name, seal, or initials does not indicate endorsement of this title. The information though satisfies all U.S. Coast Guard requirements including: 33 CFR Ch. I (7-1-00 Edition), 164.33 Charts and Publications.

Record of Corrections

Supplement No.	Notice No.	Corrected on	Corrected by

SYMBOLS ABBREVIATIONS TERMS   USED ON CHARTS

CONTENTS

INTRODUCTION
and Schematic Layout

GENERAL
- A Chart Number, Title, Marginal Notes
- B Positions, Distances, Directions, Compass

TOPOGRAPHY
- C Natural Features
- D Cultural Features
- E Landmarks
- F Ports
- G Topographic Terms

HYDROGRAPHY
- H Tides, Currents
- I Depths
- J Nature of the Seabed
- K Rocks, Wrecks, Obstructions
- L Offshore Installations
- M Tracks, Routes
- N Areas, Limits
- O Hydrographic Terms

AIDS AND SERVICES
- P Lights
- Q Buoys, Beacons
- R Fog Signals
- S Radar, Radio Electronic Position-Fixing Systems
- T Services
- U Small Craft Facilities

ALPHABETICAL INDEXES
- V Index of Abbreviations
- W International Abbreviations
- X List of Descriptors

INTRODUCTION

General Remarks—The tenth edition of Chart No. 1, Nautical Chart Symbols Abbreviations and Terms incorporates the symbols contained in the International Hydrographic Organization (IHO) Chart 1 (INT 1).The various sections comprising the Table of Contents follow the sequence presented in INT 1; therefore the numbering system in this publication follows the standard format approved and adopted by the IHO.

Where appropriate, each page lists separately the current preferred U.S. symbols shown on charts of the National Ocean Service (NOS) and the National Imagery and Mapping Agency (NIMA). Also shown in separate columns are the IHO symbols and symbols used on foreign charts reproduced by NIMA.

This edition includes a schematic layout of a typical page showing what kind of information each column presents. In addition, a typical layout of an NOS chart is shown (Section A); a page outlining tidal levels and other charted tidal data has also been included (Section H).

For more information on the use of the chart, the practice of navigation, chart sounding datum, and visual and audible aids to navigation, the user should refer to NIMA Pub. No. 9, American Practical Navigator (Bowditch).

Tide and current data is contained in the Tide Tables and Tidal Current Tables.Detailed information on lights, buoys, and beacons is available in the Coast Guard Light List and NIMA List of Lights. In addition, color plates of the U.S. Aids to Navigation System and the Uniform State Waterway Marking System are contained in the Coast Guard Light Lists.

Other important information that cannot be shown conveniently on the nautical chart can be found in the U.S. Coast Pilots and NIMA Sailing Directions.

Metric Charts and Feet/Fathom Charts—In January, 1972 the United States began producing a limited number of nautical charts in meters. Since then, some charts have been issued with soundings and contours in meters; however, for some time to come there will still be many charts on issue depicting sounding units in feet or fathoms. Modified reproductions of foreign charts are being produced retaining the sounding unit value of the country of origin. The sounding unit is stated in bold type outside the border of every chart and in the chart title

Soundings— The sounding datum reference is stated in the chart title. In all cases the unit of depth used is shown in the chart title and in the border of the chart in bold type.

Drying Heights—On rocks and banks that cover and uncover, the elevations shown are above the sounding datum, as stated in the chart title.

Shoreline— Shoreline shown on charts represents the line of contact between the land and a selected water elevation. In areas affected by tidal fluctuation, this line of contact is usually the mean high-water line. In confined coastal waters of diminished tidal influence, a mean water level line may be used. The shoreline of interior waters (rivers, lakes) is usually a line representing a specified elevation above a selected datum. Shoreline is symbolized by a heavy line (Section C1).

Apparent Shoreline is used on charts to show the outer edge of marine vegetation where that limit would reasonably appear as the shoreline to the mariner or where it prevents the shoreline from being clearly defined. Apparent shoreline is symbolized by a light line (Sections C32, C33 and C34).

Landmarks—A conspicuous feature on a building may be shown by a landmark symbol with a descriptive label (Sections E10 and E22). Prominent buildings that are of assistance to the mariner may be shown by actual shape as viewed from above (Sections D5, D6, and E34). Legends associated with landmarks, when shown in capital letters, indicate that they are conspicuous; the landmark may also be labeled "CONSPIC" or "CONSPICUOUS."

Buoys—The buoyage systems used by other countries often vary from that used by the United States. U.S. Charts show the colors, lights and other characteristics in use for the area of the individual chart. In the U.S. system, on entering a channel from seaward, buoys on the starboard side are red with even numbers, on the port side, green with odd numbers. Lights on buoys on the starboard side of the channel are red, on the port side, green. Mid-channel buoys have red and white vertical stripes and may be passed on either side. Junction or obstruction buoys have red and green horizontal bands, the top band color indicating the preferred side of passage. This system may not apply to foreign waters or in areas of the U.S. which are in IALA, Region A.

Light Visibility (Range)—(Other than on the Great Lakes and adjacent waterways.) A light's visibility (range) is given in nautical miles. Where the visibility (range) is shown as x/x M for a two (2) color light, the first number indicates the visibility (range) of the first color, while the second number indicates the visibility (range) of the second color. For example, Fl W G 12/8M indicates the visibility (range) of the white light to be 12 nautical miles and the green light to be 8 nautical miles. Where a light has three (3) colors, only the longest and shortest visibilities (ranges) may be given, in which case the middle visibility (range) is represented by a hyphen. For example, Fl W R G 12-8M indicates the visibility (range) of the white light to be 12 nautical miles, the green light to be 8 nautical miles, and the red light to be between 12 and 8 nautical miles.

IALA Buoyage System—The International Association of Lighthouse Authorities (IALA) Maritime Buoyage System (combined Cardinal-Lateral System) is being implemented by nearly every maritime buoyage jurisdiction worldwide as either REGION A buoyage (red to port) or REGION B buoyage (red to starboard). The terms "REGION A" and "REGION B" will be used to determine which type of buoyage is in effect or undergoing conversion in a particular area. The major difference in the two buoyage regions will be in the lateral marks. In REGION A they will be red to port; in REGION B they will be red to starboard. Shapes of lateral marks will be the same in both REGIONS, can to port; cone (nun) to starboard. Cardinal and other marks will continue to follow current guidelines and may be found in both REGIONS. A modified lateral mark, indicating the preferred channel where a channel divides, will be introduced for use in both REGIONS. Section Q and the color plates at the back of this publication illustrate the IALA buoyage system for both REGIONS A and B.

Aids to Navigation Positioning—The aids to navigation depicted on charts comprise a system consisting of fixed and floating aids with varying degrees of reliability. Therefore, prudent mariners will not rely solely on any single aid to navigation, particularly a floating aid.

The buoy symbol is used to indicate the approximate position of the buoy body and the sinker which secures the buoy to the seabed. The approximate position is used because of practical limitations in positioning and maintaining buoys and their sinkers in precise geographical locations. These limitations include, but are not limited to, inherent imprecisions in position fixing methods, prevailing atmospheric and sea conditions, the slope of and the material making up the seabed, the fact that buoys are moored to sinkers by varying lengths of chain, and the fact that buoy body and/or sinker positions are not under continuous surveillance but are normally checked only during periodic maintenance visits which often occur more than a year apart. The position of the buoy body can be expected to shift inside and outside the charting symbol due to the forces of nature. The mariner is also cautioned that buoys are liable to be carried away, shifted, capsized, sunk, etc. Lighted buoys may be extinguished or sound signals may not function as the result of ice, running ice, other natural causes, collisions, other accidents, or vandalism.

For the foregoing reasons a prudent mariner must not rely completely upon the position or operation of floating aids to navigation, but will also utilize bearings from fixed objects and aids to navigation on shore. Further, a vessel attempting to pass close aboard always risks collision with a yawing buoy or with the obstruction the buoy marks.

Colors—Colors are optional for characterizing various features and areas on the charts. For instance the land tint in this publication is gold as used on charts of the NOS; however, most charts of the NIMA show land tint as gray.

Heights—Heights of lights, landmarks, structures, etc. are referred to the shoreline plane of reference. Heights of small islets or offshore rocks, which due to space limitations must be placed in the water area, are bracketed. The unit of height is shown in the chart title.

Conversion Scales — Depth conversion scales are provided on all charts to enable the user to work in meters, fathoms, or feet.

Traffic Separation Schemes — Traffic separation schemes show recommended lanes to increase safety of navigation, particularly in areas of high density shipping. These schemes are described in the International Maritime Organization publication "Ships Routing".

Traffic separation schemes are generally shown on nautical charts at scales of 1:600,000 and larger. When possible, traffic separation schemes are plotted to scale and shown as depicted in Section M.

Correction Date — The date of each edition is shown below the lower left border of the chart. This is the date of the latest Notice to Mariners applied to the chart.

U.S. Coast Pilots, Sailing Directions, Light Lists, Lists of Lights —These related publications furnish information required by the navigator that cannot be shown conveniently on the nautical charts.

U.S. Nautical Chart Catalogs and Indexes — These list nautical charts, auxiliary maps, and related publications and include general information relative to the use and ordering of charts.

Corrections and Comments—Notices of Corrections for this publication will appear in the weekly Notice to Mariners. **USERS SHOULD REFER CORRECTIONS, ADDITIONS, AND COMMENTS TO THE NIMA CUSTOMER HELP DESK: 1-800-455-0899, COMMERCIAL 314-260-1236, DSN 490-1236, OR WRITE TO: DIRECTOR, NATIONAL IMAGERY AND MAPPING AGENCY, ATTN: CO, 8613 LEE HIGHWAY, FAIRFAX, VA 22031-2137.**

Schematic Layout of Chart No. 1

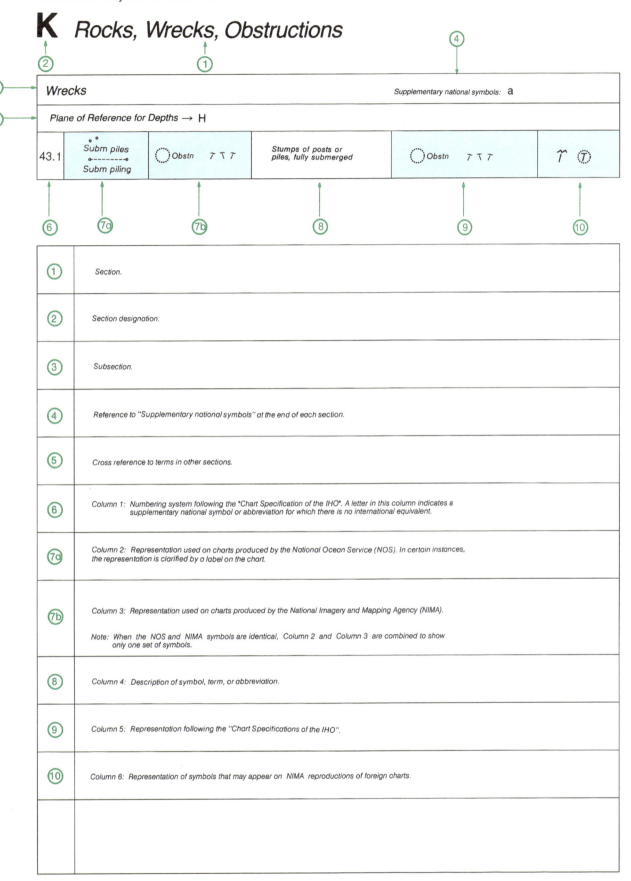

A Chart Number, Title, Marginal Notes

Schematic layout of an NOS chart (reduced in size)

DEPTHS IN METERS Nautical Chart Catalog No3 Panel I, M

INTERNATIONAL

CHART SERIES
UNITED STATES
ALASKA – SOUTH COAST
COOK INLET
Mercator Projection
Scale 1:100,000 at Lat 54°00'

Authorities

Note A

Pipelines

Caution

Submarine Operating
Area 207.640
(see note A)

Unimak Pass
1:12500

Source

Inset

(JOINS CHART INT 513)

(740,9 × 1103,9 mm)

① 412
② LORAN-C OVERPRINTED
③ INT 500

⑥ 7th Ed., June 1/96
① 412
② LORAN-C OVERPRINTED

INT 500 ③ ⑤
412 ①

ED. NO. 7
NSN 7642014009433
NIMA STOCK NO. WOBZC1

A *Chart Number, Title, Marginal Notes*

Magnetic Features → B	Tidal Data → H Decca, Loran-C, Omega → S

①	Chart number in national chart series
②	Identification of a latticed chart (if any): D for Decca LC for Loran-C Om for Omega
③	Chart number in international chart series (if any)
④	Publication note (imprint)
⑤	Bar Code and Stock Numbers
⑥	Edition note. In the example: Seventh edition published in June, 1996
⑦	Source data diagram (if any). For attention to navigators: use caution where surveys are inadequate
⑧	Dimensions of inner borders
⑨	Corner co-ordinates
⑩	Chart title } May be quoted when ordering a chart, in addition to chart number
⑪	Explanatory notes on chart construction, etc. To be read before using chart
⑫	Seals: In the example, the national and International Hydrographic Organization seals show that this national chart is also an international one. Purely national charts have the national seal only. Reproductions of charts of other nations (facsimile) have the seals of the original producer (left), publisher (center) and the IHO (right)
⑬	Projection and scale of chart at stated latitude. The scale is precisely as stated only at the latitude quoted
⑭	Linear scale on large-scale charts
⑮	Reference to a larger-scale chart
⑯	Cautionary notes (if any). Information on particular features, to be read before using chart
⑰	Reference to an adjoining chart of similar scale

B Positions, Distances, Directions, Compass

Geographical Positions

1	Lat	Latitude	Lat
2	Long	Longitude	Long
3		International meridian (Greenwich)	
4	°	Degree(s)	°
5	′	Minute(s) of arc	′
6	″	Second(s) of arc	″
7	PA	Position approximate	PA
8	PD	Position doubtful	PD
9	N	North, Northern	N
10	E	East, Eastern	E
11	S	South, Southern	S
12	W	West, Western	W
13	NE	Northeast	NE
14	SE	Southeast	SE
15	NW	Northwest	NW
16	SW	Southwest	SW

Control Points

20	△	Triangulation point	△
21	⊕ Obs Spot	Observation spot	⊕
22	⊙	Fixed point	⊙
23	○ BM	Benchmark	⊤
24	◇ Bdy Mon	Boundary mark	

Symbolized Positions (Examples)

30	# 〈18〉 Wk (PA)	Symbols in plan: position is center of primary symbol	⌂ # 〈18〉 Wk (PA)
31	⊥ ₽	Symbols in profile: position is at bottom of symbol	⚑ ⊥ ₽ ₽
32	⊙	Point symbols (accurate positions)	⊙ Mast ⊙ MAST ☆
33	○	Approximate position	○ Mast PA

B *Positions, Distances, Directions, Compass*

Units			*Supplementary national symbols:* a – m	
40	km	Kilometer(s)	km	
41	m	Meter(s)	m	
42	dm	Decimeter(s)	dm	
43	cm	Centimeter(s)	cm	
44	mm	Millimeter(s)	mm	
45	M, Mi, NMi, NM	Nautical mile(s) (1852 m) or sea mile(s)	M	
46	cbl	Cable(s) length		
47	ft	Foot/feet	ft	
48	fm, fms	Fathom(s)		
49	h, hr	Hour	h	
50	m, min	Minute(s) of time	m	min
51	s, sec	Second(s) of time	s	sec
52	kn	Knot(s)	kn	
53	t	Ton(s) (metric ton equals 2,204.6 lbs)	t	
54	cd	Candela (new candle)	cd	
Magnetic Compass			*Supplementary national symbols:* n	
60	var VAR	Variation		
61	mag	magnetic		
62	brg	Bearing		
63	T	true		
64		decreasing		
65		increasing		
66		Annual change		
67	dev	Deviation		
68.1		Note of magnetic variation, in position	Magnetic Variation 4°31'W 1995 (8'E)	
68.2		Note of magnetic variation, out of position	Magnetic Variation at 55°N 8°W 4°31'W 1995 (8'E)	

B *Positions, Distances, Directions, Compass*

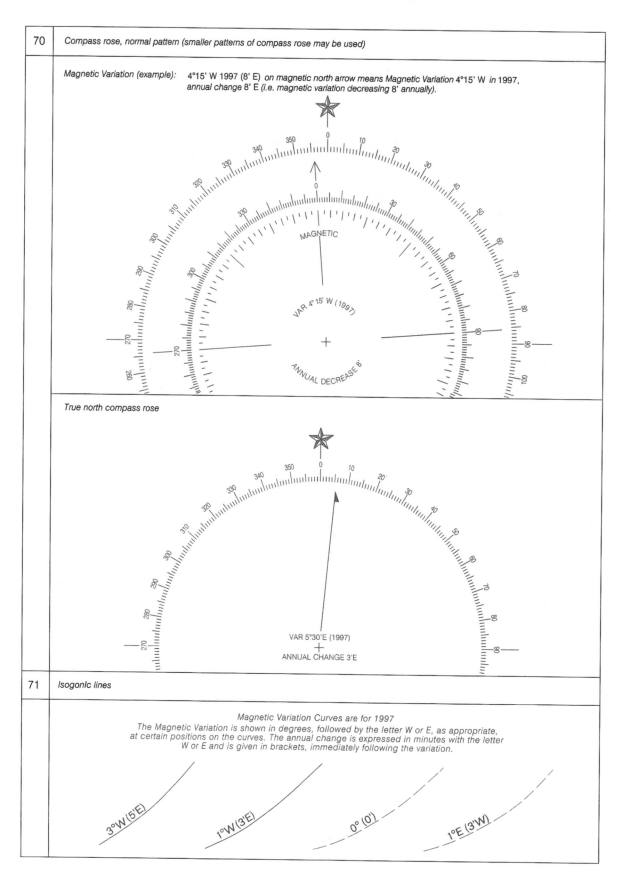

B Positions, Distances, Directions, Compass

82.1	+15° (enclosed shape)	Local magnetic disturbance Within the enclosed area the magnetic variation may deviate from the normal by the value shown	±15° (enclosed shape)
82.2	Local Magnetic Disturbance (see Note)	Where the area affected cannot be easily defined, a legend only is shown at the position	Local Magnetic Anomaly (see Note)

Supplementary National Symbols

a	m²	Square meter	
b	m³	Cubic meter	
c	in, ins	Inch(es)	
d	yd, yds	Yard(s)	
e	St M, St Mi	Statute mile	
f	μsec, μs	Microsecond	
g	Hz	Hertz	
h	kHz	Kilohertz	
i	MHz	Megahertz	
j	cps, c/s	Cycles/second	
k	kc	Kilocycle	
l	Mc	Megacycle	
m	T	Ton (U.S. short ton equals 2,000 lbs)	
n	deg	Degree(s)	

C Natural Features

Coastline

Supplementary national symbols: a – e

Foreshore → I, J

1		Coastline, surveyed	
2		Coastline, unsurveyed	
3	high / low	Steep coast, Steep coast with rock cliffs, Cliffs	
4		Coastal hillocks, elevation not determined	
5		Flat coast	
6		Sandy shore	
7		Stony shore, Shingly shore	Stones
8		Sandhills, Dunes	Dunes
9	Marsh	Apparent Shoreline	
9.1		Vegetation or topographic Feature Area Limit in general	

14

C Natural Features

Relief

Supplementary national symbols: f, g

Plane of Reference for Heights → H

10		Contour lines with spot height	
11	· 256	Spot heights	
12		Approximate contour lines with approximate height	
13		Form lines with spot height	
14		Approximate height of top of trees (above height datum)	

Water Features, Lava

Supplementary national symbols: h

20		River, Stream	
21		Intermittent river	
22		Rapids, Waterfalls	
23		Lakes	

C Natural Features

24		Salt pans	
25		Glacier	
26		Lava flow	

Vegetation			Supplementary national symbols: i - o
30	Wooded	Wood, in general	Wooded
31		Prominent trees (in groups or isolated)	
31.1		Deciduous tree	
31.2		Evergreen (except conifer)	
31.3		Conifer	
31.4		Palm	
31.5		Nipa palm	
31.6		Casuarina	
31.7		Filao	
31.8		Eucalyptus	

C Natural Features

32	Mangrove (used in small areas)	Mangrove	
33	Marsh (used in small areas) / Swamp	Marsh / Swamp	Marsh
34	Cypress	Cypress	

Supplementary National Symbols			
a	Uncovers	Chart sounding datum line (surveyed)	
b		Approximate sounding datum line (inadequately surveyed)	
c	Mud	Foreshore; Strand (in general) Stones; Shingle; Gravel; Mud; Sand	
d	Breakers (if extensive)	Breakers along a shore	

C Natural Features

e		Rubble	
f		Hachures	
g		Shading	
h		Lagoon	
i	Wooded	Deciduous woodland	
j	Wooded	Coniferous woodland	
k		Tree plantation	
l	Cultivated	Cultivated fields	
m	Grass	Grass fields	
n	Rice	Paddy (rice) fields	
o	Bushes	Bushes	

D Cultural Features

Settlements, Buildings

Height of objects → E   Landmarks → E

1		Urban area	
2		Settlement with scattered buildings	
3		Settlement (on medium and small-scale charts)	○ Name ▭ Name
4	Vil	Village	✠ Name ■ Name HOTEL
5		Buildings in general	
6		Important building in built-up area	Hotel Hotel
7	Church Street	Street name, Road name — St Street, Ave Avenue, Blvd Boulevard	N A M E
8	Ruins ○ Ru	Ruins, Ruined landmark	Ru Ru

Roads, Railways, Airfields

Supplementary national symbols: a-c

10		Motorway
11		Road (hard surfaced)
12		Track, Path (loose or unsurfaced)
13		Railway, with station
14		Cutting

D Cultural Features

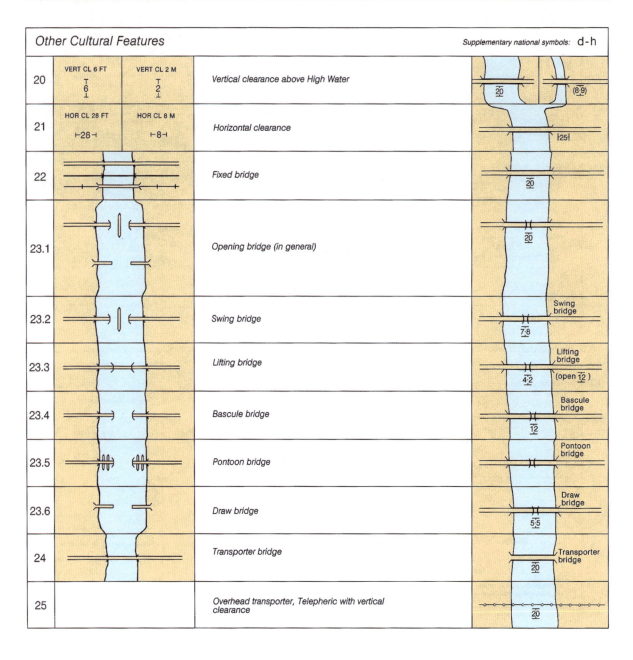

D Cultural Features

26	OVERHEAD POWER CABLE AUTHORIZED CL 140 FT / TOWER TOWER	Power transmission line with pylons and safe overhead clearance	Pyl — s — ⊙ — s — Pyl — ⊙ — s / s 20 s
27	Tel	Overhead cable, Telephone line, Telegraph line	20
28	OVHD PIPE VERT CL 6 FT	Overhead pipe with vertical clearance	Overhead pipe / 20
29		Pipeline on land	

	Supplementary National Symbols		
a	20 50 95	Highway markers	
b	CONRAIL / Same grade / Ry above / Ry below	Railway (Ry) (single or double track) Railroad (RR)	
c	+ + + + + + +	Abandoned railroad	
d		Bridge under construction	
e		Footbridge	
f	Viaduct	Viaduct	
g		Fence	
h		Power transmission line	

21

E Landmarks

Plane of reference for Heights → H		Lighthouses → P		Beacons → Q
General				
1	⊙TANK ₒTk ⊕ ⌀	Examples of landmarks	◆ Building ₒ Hotel	
2	⊙ CAPITOL DOME ⊙ WORLD TRADE CENTER	Examples of conspicuous landmarks	◆ FACTORY WATER TR ⊙ HOTEL WATER TOWER	
3.1		Pictorial symbols (in true position)	🏢 🏢	
3.2		Sketches, Views (out of position)	🏠 🏭	
4	(30)	Height of top of a structure above plane of reference for heights	(30)	
5	(30)	Height of structure above ground level	(30)	
Landmarks				
10.1	✚ Ch	Church	✚ ⛪ Ch	✦ ✝
10.2		Church tower	✚ Tr ⛪ Tr	
10.3	⊙SPIRE ₒSpire	Church spire	✚ Sp ⛪ Sp	✝ ✝ ✝
10.4	⊙CUPOLA ₒCup	Church cupola	✚ Cup ⛪ Cup	♀
11	✚ Ch	Chapel		✝
12	✝	Cross, Calvary		+ ✝
13	⊠	Temple	⊠	⊕
14	⊠	Pagoda	⊠	
15	⊠	Shinto shrine, Josshouse	⊠	卍

E Landmarks

16		⊠	Buddhist temple	⊠ 卍	
17		Ö ö ⩑	Mosque, Minaret	ö	⩑ ö
18		⊡ ö	Marabout	⊚ Marabout	
19	▭ Cem	⊞ / Cem	Cemetery (for all religious denominations)	L L L L L L L L L	▭ u u u
20	⊙ TOWER ○ Tr		Tower	🯅 Tr	
21	⊙ STANDPIPE ○ S'pipe	⊙ WTR TR ○ Wtr Tr	Standpipe Water tower, Water tank on a tower	🯅	
22	⊙ CHIMNEY ○ Chy		Chimney	🯅 ◣ Chy	🯅
23	⊙ FLARE ○ Flare		Flare stack (on land)	🯅	
24	⊙ MONUMENT ○ Mon		Monument	🯅 Mon	🯅 ⚭
25.1	⊙ WINDMILL ○ Windmill	⊙ WINDMILL ⊗	Windmill	✕	☥ ⚹
25.2			Windmill (wingless)	✕ Ru	
26	⊙ WINDMOTOR ○ Windmotor		Windmotor	🯅	⊗ ✕
27	⊙ F S ○ F S	⊙ F P ○ F P	Flagstaff, Flagpole	🯅 FS	
28	⊙ R MAST ○ R Mast	⊙ TV MAST ○ TV Mast	Radio mast, Television mast	🯅	
29	⊙ R TR ○ R Tr	⊙ TV TR ○ TV Tr	Radio tower, Television tower	🯅	
30.1	⊙ RADAR MAST ○ Radar Mast		Radar mast	⊚ Radar Mast	

23

E Landmarks

30.2	⊙ RADAR TR ∘ Radar Tr		Radar tower	⊙ Radar Tr	
30.3			Radar scanner	⊙ Radar Sc	
30.4	⊙ DOME(RADAR) ∘ Dome (Radar)	⊙ RADOME ∘ Radome	Radar dome	⊙ Radome	
31	⊙ ANT (RADAR) ∘ Ant (Radar)		Dish aerial		
32	⊙ TANK ∘ Tk ⊘		Tanks	• ⊕ Tanks	
33	⊙ SILO ∘ Silo	⊙ ELEVATOR ∘ Elevator	Silo, Elevator	○ Silo ⊙ Silo	
34.1			Fortified structure (on large-scale charts)		
34.2	Cas		Castle, Fort, Blockhouse (on smaller-scale charts)		✠
34.3			Battery, Small fort (on smaller-scale charts)		
35.1			Quarry (on large-scale charts)		
35.2	⚒		Quarry (on smaller-scale charts)	⚒	⚱
36	⚒		Mine	⚒	

Supplementary National Symbols				
a		Moslem Shrine		
b		Tomb		

E Landmarks

c		Watermill		☼
d	▨ ▪ ▯ Facty	Factory		
e	○ Well	Well		
f	▪ Sch	School		
g	▪ Hosp	Hospital		
h	▪ Univ	University		
i	⊙ GAB ○ Gab	Gable		
j	⋀	Camping site		
k	Tel Tel Off	Telegraph Telegraph office		
l	Magz	Magazine		
m	Govt Ho	Government house		
n	Inst	Institute		
o	Ct Ho	Courthouse		
p	Pav	Pavilion		
q	T	Telephone		
r	Ltd	Limited		
s	Apt	Apartment		
t	Cap	Capitol		
u	Co	Company		
v	Corp	Corporation		

F Ports

Hydraulic Structures in General

Supplementary national symbols: a–c

1		Dike, Levee
2.1		Seawall (on large-scale charts)
2.2		Seawall (on smaller-scale charts)
3	Cswy	Causeway
4.1	Bkw	Breakwater (in general)
4.2		Breakwater (loose boulders, tetrapods, etc.)
4.3		Breakwater (slope of concrete or masonry)
5	Training wall	Training wall (partly submerged at high water)
6.1	Groin	Groin (always dry)
6.2	Groin	Groin (intertidal)
6.3	Groin	Groin (always under water)

Harbor Installations

Depths → I   Anchorages, Limits → N   Beacons and other fixed marks → Q   Marina → U

10	Fishing harbor	

26

F Ports

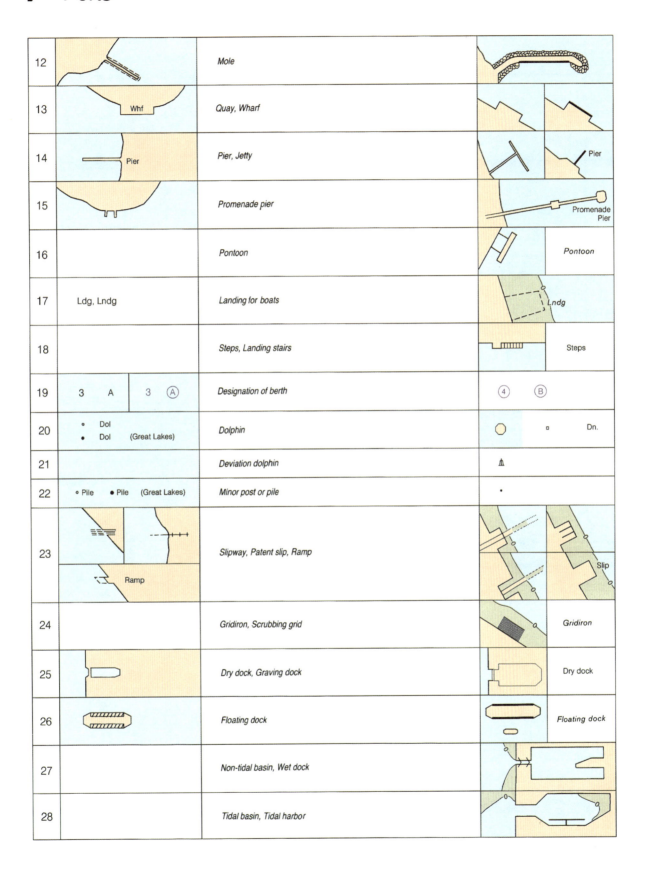

F Ports

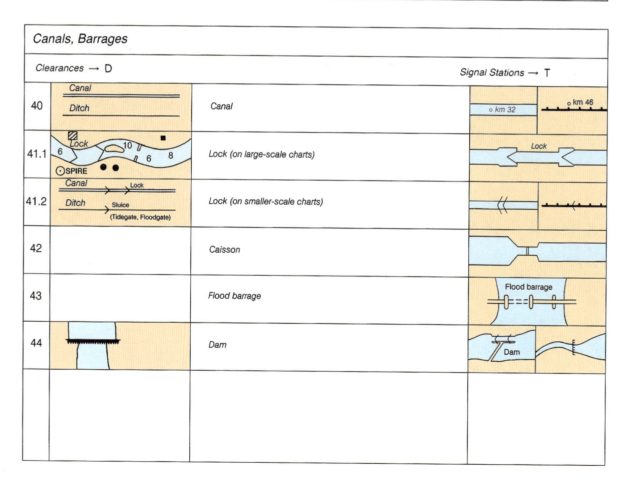

28

F Ports

Transishipment Facilities

Supplementary national symbol : d

	Roads → D		Railways → D	Tanks → E
50		RoRo	Roll-on. Roll-off Ferry (Ro Ro Terminal)	RoRo
51			Transit shed. Warehouse (with designation)	
52	⊙		Timber yard	♯
53.1	⊙	⊙ (4t)	Crane with lifting capacity. crane (on railway)	(3 t)
53.2	⊙	⊙ (14t)	Container crane with lifting capacity	(50 t)
53.3			Sheerlegs (conspicuous)	⊙ SHEERLEGS

Public Buildings

Supplementary national abbreviation : e

60	Hbr Mr	Harbormaster's office	⚓
61	■ Cus Ho	Customhouse	⊖
62.1	⊕ Health Office	Health officer's office	⊕
62.2	■ Hosp	Hospital	⊕ Hospital
63	■ PO	Post office	✉

Supplementary National Symbols

a		Jetty (partly below MHW)	
b		Submerged jetty	
c		Jetty (small scale)	
d	ⓟ	Pump-out facilities	
e	⊕ Quar	Quarantine	

G Topographic Terms

Coast

1	Island	8	Head, Headland
2	Islet	9	Point
3	Cay	10	Spit
4	Peninsula	11	Rock
5	Archipelago	12	Salt marsh, Saltings
6	Atoll	13	Lagoon
7	Cape		

Natural Inland-Features

20	Promontory	30	Plateau
21	Range	31	Valley
22	Ridge	32	Ravine, Cut
23	Mountain, Mount	33	Gorge
24	Summit	34	Vegetation
25	Peak	35	Grassland
26	Volcano	36	Paddy field
27	Hill	37	Bushes
28	Boulder	38	Deciduous woodland
29	Table-land	39	Coniferous woodland

Settlements

50	City, Town	53	Farm
51	Village	54	Saint
52	Fishing village		

Buildings

60	Structure	62	Hut
61	House		

G Topographic Terms

63	Multi-story building		82	Cement works
64	Castle		83	Water mill
65	Pyramid		84	Greenhouse
66	Column		85	Warehouse, Storehouse
67	Mast		86	Cold store, Refrigerating storage house
68	Lattice tower		87	Refinery
69	Mooring mast		88	Power station
70	Floodlight		89	Electric works
71	Town hall		90	Gas works
72	Office		91	Water works
73	Observatory		92	Sewage works
74	Institute		93	Machine house, Pump house
75	Cathedral		94	Well
76	Monastery, Convent		95	Telegraph office
77	Lookout station, Watch tower		96	Hotel
78	Navigation school		97	Sailors' home
79	Naval college		98	Spa hotel
80	Factory			
81	Brick kiln, Brick works			

Road, Rail and Air Traffic

110	Street, Road		116	Runway
111	Avenue		117	Landing lights
112	Tramway		118	Helicopter landing site
113	Viaduct			
114	Suspension bridge			
115	Footbridge			

Ports, Harbors

130	Tidal barrier		132	Loading canal
131	Boat lift, Ship lift, Hoist		133	Sluice

G Topographic Terms

134	Basin	147	Commercial port, Trade port
135	Reservoir	148	Building harbor
136	Reclamation area	149	Oil harbor
137	Port	150	Ore harbor
138	Harbor	151	Grain harbor
139	Haven	152	Container harbor
140	Inner harbor	153	Timber harbor
141	Outer harbor	154	Coal harbor
142	Deep water harbor	155	Ferry harbor
143	Free port	156	Police
144	Customs harbor		
145	Naval port		
146	Industrial harbor		

Harbor Installations

170	Terminal	185	Liquified Natural Gas LNG
171	Building slip	186	Liquified Petroleum Gas LPG
172	Building yard	187	Very Large Crude Carrier VLCC
173	Buoy yard, Buoy dump		
174	Bunker station		
175	Reception facilities for oily wastes		
176	Tanker cleaning facilities		
177	Cooling water intake/outfall		
178	Floating barrier Boom		
179	Piling		
180	Row of piles		
181	Bollard		
182	Conveyor		
183	Storage tanker		
184	Lighter Aboard Ship - LASH		

H Tides, Currents

Terms Relating to Tidal Levels			Supplementary national symbols: a-k
1		Chart Datum, Datum for sounding reduction	CD
2		Lowest Astronomical Tide	LAT
3		Highest Astronomical Tide	HAT
4	MLW	Mean Low Water	MLW
5	MHW	Mean High Water	MHW
6	MSL	Mean Sea Level	MSL
7		Land survey datum	
8	MLWS	Mean Low Water Springs	MLWS
9	MHWS	Mean High Water Springs	MHWS
10	MLWN	Mean Low Water Neaps	MLWN
11	MHWN	Mean High Water Neaps	MHWN
12	MLLW	Mean Lower Low Water	MLLW
13	MHHW	Mean Higher High Water	MHHW
14		Mean Higher Low Water	MHLW
15		Mean Lower High Water	MLHW
16	Sp	Spring tide	Sp
17	Np	Neap tide	Np

H Tides, Currents

Tidal Levels and charted Data — Tide gauge → T

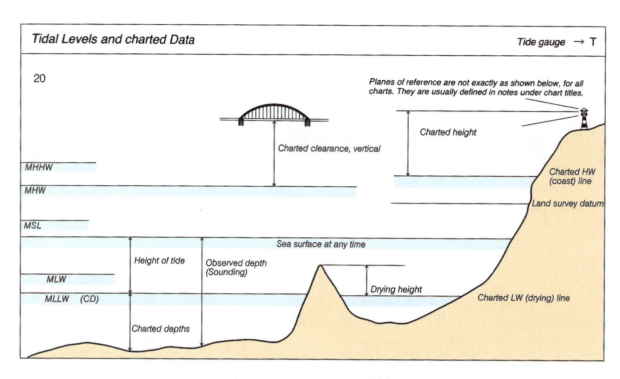

20

Tide Tables

30 — Tidal Levels referred to Datum of Soundings

Place	Lat N/S	Long E/W	Heights in meters above datum			
			MHWS	MHWN	MLWN	MLWS
			MHHW	MLHW	MHLW	MLLW

Tabular statement of semi-diurnal or diurnal tides

Note: The order of the columns of levels will be the same as that used in national tables of tidal predictions.

31 — Tidal stream table

Tidal streams referred to..

34

H Tides, Currents

Tidal Streams and Currents

Supplementary national symbols: m-t

Breakers → K   Tide Gauge → T

40	2 kn →	Flood stream (current) with rate	2.5 kn →
41	2 kn →	Ebb stream (current) with rate	2.5 kn →
42		Current in restricted waters	»»»» →
43		Ocean current with rates and seasons	2.5-4.5 kn Jan–Mar (see Note)
44	Tide rips *Symbol used only in small areas*	Overfalls, tide rips, races	
45	Eddies *Symbol used only in small areas*	Eddies	
46	Ⓐ Ⓑ	Position of tabulated tidal data with designation	Ⓐ

Supplementary National Symbols

a	HW	High water	
b	HHW	Higher high water	
c	LW	Low water	
d	LWD	Low-water datum	
e	LLW	Lower low water	
f	MTL	Mean tide level	
g	ISLW	Indian spring low water	
h	HWF&C	High-water full and change (vulgar establishment of the port)	
i	LWF&C	Low-water full and change	

35

H Tides, Currents

j	CRD	Columbia River Datum	
k	GCLWD	Gulf Coast Low Water Datum	
l	Str	Stream	
m	2kn →	Current, general, with rate	
n	vel	Velocity; Rate	
o	kn	Knots	
p	ht	Height	
q	fl	Flood	
r	●	New moon	
s	☺	Full moon	
t	(compass diagram)	Current diagram	

Depths

		General		
1	ED	Existence doubtful		ED
2	SD	Sounding doubtful		SD
3.1	Rep	Reported, but not surveyed		Rep
3.2	(3) Rep (1983)	Reported with year of report, but not surveyed		Rep (1973)
4	(3) Rep	Reported but not confirmed sounding or danger		(184) (212)

Soundings

Supplementary national symbols: a - c

Plane of Reference for Depths → H   Plane of Reference for Heights → H

10	19 8_2 $6\frac{3}{4}$ 8_2 19	19 8_2 $6\frac{3}{4}$	Sounding in true position (NOS uses upright soundings on English unit charts and sloping soundings on Metric charts).	12 9_7
11	(23) $\cdot^{-1036}$		Sounding out of position	+(12) 3375
12		(5)	Least depth in narrow channel	(9_7)
13	$\overline{65}$		No bottom found at depth shown	$\overline{200}$
14	8_2 19 8_2 19	8_2 19	Soundings which are unreliable or taken from a smaller-scale source (NOS uses sloping soundings on English unit charts and upright soundings on Metric charts).	12 9_7
15	6		Drying heights above chart datum	4_9 0_9 4_7 3_6 4 2 3_8

I Depths

Depths in Fairways and Areas

Supplementary national symbols: a, b

Plane of Reference for Depths → H

20		Limit of dredged area		
21	7.0 m	Dredged channel or area with depth of dredging in meters	7.0 m	7.0 meters
22	24 FEET OCT 1983 / 30 FEET APR 1984	Dredged channel or area with depth and year of the latest control survey	Dredged to 7.2m (1978)	7.2m (1978)
23	Maintained depth 7.2m	Dredged channel or area with maintained depth	Maintained depth 7.2m	7.2m
24		Depth at chart datum, to which an area has been swept by wire drag. The latest date of sweeping may be shown in parentheses	10_2 10_8 9_6 (1980) 11 9_8	
25	Sand and mud / Unsurveyed	Unsurveyed or inadequately surveyed area; area with inadequate depth information	Inadequately Surveyed (see Note) / Inadequately Surveyed (see Note)	

Depths

Depth Contours

	Feet	Fm/Meters
	0	0
	6	1
	12	2
	18	3
	24	4
	30	5
	36	6
	60	10
	120	20
	180	30
	240	40
	300	50
	600	100
	1,200	200
	1,800	300
	2,400	400
	3,000	500
	6,000	1,000

30

Low water line

One or two lighter blue tints may be used instead of the 'ribbons' of tint at 10 or 20 m

31 — Approximate depth contour — Continuous lines, with values (black ——100—— blue or)

Approximate depth contours

Note: The extent of the blue tint varies with the scale and purpose of the chart, or its sources. On some charts, contours and figures are printed in blue.

Supplementary National Symbols

a	----6----	Swept channel
b	89 17 / 119 15	Swept area, not adequately sounded (shown by purple or green tint)
c	6—5— 2 ft	Stream

J Nature of the Seabed

Types of Seabed

Rocks → K   Supplementary national abbreviations: a–ag

1	S	Sand	S
2	M	Mud	M
3	Cy; Cl	Clay	Cy
4	Si	Silt	Si
5	St	Stones	St
6	G	Gravel	G
7	P	Pebbles	P
8	Cb	Cobbles	Cb
9	Rk; rky	Rock; Rocky	R
10	Co	Coral and Coralline algae	Co
11	Sh	Shells	Sh
12	S/M	Two layers, eg. Sand over mud	S/M
13.1	Wd	Weed (including Kelp)	Wd
13.2	Kelp	Kelp, Seaweed	
14	Sandwaves	Mobile bottom (sand waves)	
15	Spring	Freshwater springs in seabed	T

Types of Seabed, Intertidal Areas

20	Gravel	Area with stones, gravel or shingle	G St
21	Rock	Rocky area, which covers and uncovers	
22	Coral	Coral reef, which covers and uncovers	

J Nature of the Seabed

Qualifying Terms

Supplementary national abbreviations: ah - bf

30	f; fne	fine		f
31	m	medium	only used in relation to sand	m
32	c; crs	coarse		c
33	bk; brk	broken		bk
34	sy; stk	sticky		sy
35	so; sft	soft		so
36	stf	stiff		sf
37	Vol	volcanic		v
38	Ca	calcareous		ca
39	h; hrd	hard		h

Supplementary National Abbreviations

a	Grd		Ground	
b	Oz		Ooze	
c	Ml		Marl	
d	Sn		Shingle	
e	Blds		Boulders	
f	Ck		Chalk	
g	Qz		Quartz	
h	Sch		Schist	
i	Co Hd		Coral head	
j	Mds		Madrepores	
k	Vol Ash		Volcanic ash	
l	La		Lava	
m	Pm		Pumice	
n	T		Tufa	
o	Sc		Scoriae	
p	Cn		Cinders	
q	Mn		Manganese	
r	Oys		Oysters	
s	Ms		Mussels	
t	Spg		Sponge	
u	K		Kelp	
v	Grs		Grass	
w	Stg		Sea-tangle	
x	Spi		Spicules	
y	Fr		Foraminifera	
z	Gl		Globigerina	
aa	Di		Diatoms	

J *Nature of the Seabed*

ab	Rd		Radiolaria	
ac	Pt		Pteropods	
ad	Po		Polyzoa	
ae	Cir		Cirripedia	
af	Fu		Fucus	
ag	Ma		Mattes	
ah	sml		Small	
ai	lrg		Large	
aj	rt		Rotten	
ak	str		Streaky	
al	spk		Speckled	
am	gty		Gritty	
an	dec		Decayed	
ao	fly		Flinty	
ap	glac		Glacial	
aq	ten		Tenacious	
ar	wh		White	
as	bl; bk		Black	
at	vi		Violet	
au	bu		Blue	
av	gn		Green	
aw	yl		Yellow	
ax	or		Orange	
ay	rd		Red	
az	br		Brown	
ba	ch		Chocolate	
bb	gy		Gray	
bc	lt		Light	
bd	dk		Dark	
be	vard		Varied	
bf	unev		Uneven	

K Rocks, Wrecks, Obstructions

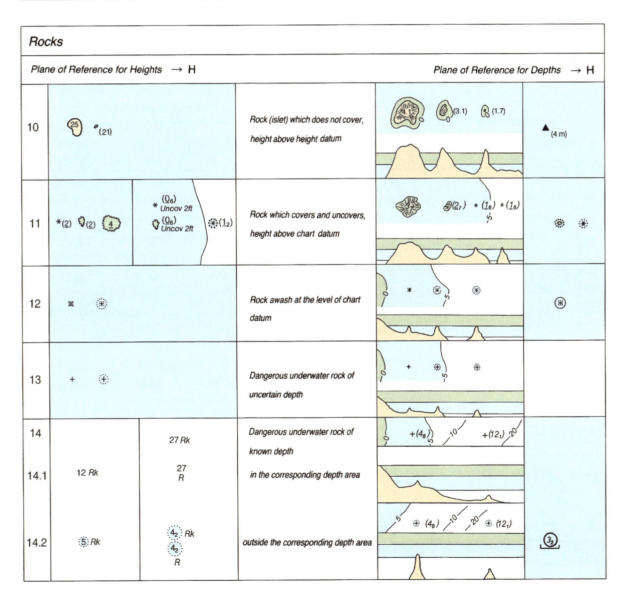

43

K Rocks, Wrecks, Obstructions

15	+ 35 Rk	35 Rk 35 R	Non-dangerous rock, depth known	21 R	35 R. 35 R + (35)
16	+Co 3₁ +	Reef line	Coral reef which covers	+Co + + +Co	
17	Breakers	Br	Breakers		⑤₈ Br 19 18

Wrecks

Plane of Reference for Depths → H

20	⬭ Hk		Wreck, hull always dry, on large-scale charts	Wk	
21	⬭> Hk		Wreck, covers and uncovers, on large-scale charts	Wk	Wk Wk Wk Wk
22			Submerged wreck, depth known, on large-scale charts	5₂ Wk	⊂9⊃ Wk
23		⊂ ⊃> Hk	Submerged wreck, depth unknown, on large-scale charts	Wk	Wk Wk
24	⊼		Wreck showing any portion of hull or superstructure at level of chart datum	⊼	Wk Wk
25	⊞ Masts Mast (10 ft) Funnel ⊞ Masts		Wreck showing mast or masts above chart datum only	⊞ Mast	
26	5₁ Wk	5₂ Wk	Wreck, least depth known by sounding only	4₆ Wk 25 Wk	⊞ (9)
27	21 Wk 5 Wk	4₆ Wk	Wreck, least depth known, swept by wire drag or diver	4₆ Wk 25 Wk	+++ 21 Rk
28	⊞		Dangerous wreck, depth unknown	⊞	
29	+++		Sunken wreck, not dangerous to surface navigation	+++	
30	8 Wk	25 Wk	Wreck, least depth unknown, but considered to have a safe clearance to the depth shown	25 Wk	15

K Rocks, Wrecks, Obstructions

31	Foul # Foul	Foul ground, non-dangerous to navigation but to be avoided by vessels anchoring, trawling etc.	# Foul # / ⒻⒷ
32	Foul / Wks / Wreckage	Foul area, Foul with rocks or wreckage, dangerous to navigation.	

Obstructions

Plane of Reference for Depths → H   Kelp, Sea-Weed → J

40	Obstn Obstn	Obstruction, depth unknown	Obstn Obstn #
41	5¼ Obstn 5₂ Obstn	Obstruction, least depth known	4₆ Obstn 16₈ Obstn
42	21 Obstn / 5 Obstn 4₈ Obstn	Obstruction, least depth known, swept by wire drag or diver	4₆ Obstn 16₈ Obstn
43.1	Subm piles Stakes, Perches Obstn т т т	Stumps of posts or piles, all or part of the time submerged	Obstn т т т ⊤ Ⓣ Subm piles
43.2	∘∘ Snags ∘∘ Stumps ∘∘ Deadhead	Submerged pile, stake, snag, well, deadhead or stump (with exact position)	⌇ ⌇ ⊤ Ⓣ
44.1	⊔⊔⊔⊔⊔⊔⊔⊔⊔ Fsh stks	Fishing stakes	⊔⊔⊔ ⊔⊔⊔
44.2	▭--) ▱	Fish trap, fish weirs, tunny nets	▱
45	─── ───	Fish traps	Tunny nets	Fish trap area, tunny nets area		Fish traps		Tunny nets	
46.1	Obstruction (fish haven) (actual shape) Obstn (fish haven)	Fish haven (artificial fishing reef)	🐟 🐟
46.2	Obstn Fish haven (Auth min 42ft) 🐟	Fish haven with minimum depth	🐟 (2₄) 🐟 2₄
47	(Oys)	Shellfish cultivation (stakes visible)	Shellfish Beds (see Note)

45

K Rocks, Wrecks, Obstructions

	Supplementary National Symbols				
a	∗ ✳		Rock awash (height unknown)		
b	⑤ Rk ⑤ Rks		Shoal sounding on isolated rock or rocks		⑨ R ② r ② P ⊕(8)
c	⊞		Sunken wreck covered 20 to 30 meters		⊞
d	◯ Sub vol		Submarine volcano		
e	◯ Discol water		Discolored water		
f	21 Rk 3₂ 3₂		Sunken danger with depth cleared (swept) by wire drag		Obstn 21 5
g	Reef		Reef of unknown extent		
h	✳ Co	Coral Co ⌵Co ✳Co	Coral reef, detached (uncovers at sounding datum)		
i	▢ Subm Crib	▢ Crib	Submerged Crib		□
j	□ Crib	□ Duck Blind	Crib, Duck Blind (above water)		
k	▢ Duck Blind		Submerged Duck Blind		
l	▢ Platform		Submerged Platform		

L Offshore Installations

Offshore Installations					
General					
Areas, Limits → N					
1		DURRAH OILFIELD	Name of oilfield or gasfield	Oil field	
2	▪ "Hazel"	"Hazel"	Platform with designation/name	Z-44	
3			Limit of safety zone around offshore installation		
4			Limit of development area		

Platforms and Moorings					
Mooring Buoys → Q					
10	▪ "Exxon MP−236"		Production platform, Platform, Oil derrick		
11			Flare stack (at sea)	Fla	
12		SPM	Mooring tower, Articulated Loading Platform (ALP), Single Anchor Leg Mooring (SALM)	SPM	
13	▪ "Hazel"	"Tuna"	Observation/research platform (with name)		
14			Disused platform		
15	Artificial Island (Mukluk)		Artificial island		
16			Oil or Gas installation buoy, Catenary Anchor Leg Mooring (CALM), Single Buoy Mooring (SBM)		
17		Tanker	Moored storage tanker		

47

L Offshore Installations

Underwater Installations

Supplementary national symbols: a

Plane of Reference for Depths → H   Obstructions → K

20	Well (cov 21ft) / Well (cov 83ft)	Well	Submerged production well	Prod. Well	
21.1	Pipe	Well	Suspended well, depth over wellhead unknown	Well	
21.2	Pipe (cov 24ft) / Pipe (cov 92ft)	15 Well	Suspended well, with depth over wellhead	15 Well	
21.3			Wellhead with height above the bottom	Well (5.7)	
22			Site of cleared platform	#	
23	Pipe		Above water wellheads	Pipe	

Submarine Cables

30.1	~~~~~		Submarine cable	~~~~~	
30.2	Cable Area		Submarine cable area		
31.1	~S~S~S~		Submarine power cable	~S~S~	
31.2		~T~T~S~T~	Submarine power cable area	~T~T~S~T~T~	
32	~ ~ ~ ~ ~		Disused submarine cable	~ ~ ~ ~	

L Offshore Installations

Submarine Pipelines

40.1		Oil, Gas pipeline	Oil (see note) / Gas (see note)	
40.2	Pipeline Area	Oil, Gas pipeline areas	Oil (see note) / Gas (see note)	
41.1	Water / Sewer / Outfall / Intake	Waterpipe, sewer, outfall pipe, intake pipe	Water / Sewer / Outfall / Intake	
41.2	Pipeline Area	Discharge pipeline areas	Water / Sewer / Outfall / Intake	
42		Buried pipeline/pipe (with nominal depth to which buried)	Buried 1.6m	
43	PWI / Depth over Crib 17ft / Crib	Potable Water intake, diffuser, or crib	3_2 Obstn	
44		Disused pipeline/pipe		

Supplementary National Symbol

a	Well Well Well	Submerged well (buoyed)		

M Tracks, Routes

Tracks

Tracks Marked by Lights → P   *Leading Beacons → Q*   Supplementary national symbols: a — c

1	——— — — — —	Lights in line 090°	Leading line (solid line is fairway)	2 Bns ╪ 270.5° / 2 Bns ╪ 270°30'
2		Beacons in line 090°	Transit, clearing line	2 Bns ╪ 270°30' / 2 Bns ╪ 270.5°
3	——— ———	Lights in line 090°	Recommended track based on a system of fixed marks	2 Bns ╪ 090.5°–270.5° / --> --> --
4	--<-->-- / --<-->--		Recommended tracks not based on a system of fixed marks	———— 090.5°–270.5° / ——<-->——
5.1	--> -- > --		One-way track	☆-----☆ ⇐ / ——<———<—
5.2			Two-way track (including a regulation described in a note)	☆-----☆ SEE NOTE / -<-->SEE NOTE<-->-
6		——‹7m›— / ——‹7₃m›——	Track, recommended track with maximum authorized draft stated	——‹7.0m›—— / ——‹7.3m›——

Routing Measures

Basic Symbols

Supplementary national symbols: d — e

10	⇒	Established (mandatory) direction of traffic flow	⇒
11	===⇒	Recommended direction of traffic flow	===⇒
12	▬▬▬	Separation line	▬▬▬
13	▬ ▬▬	Separation zone	▬▬▬
14	RESTRICTED AREA ⊥⊥⊥⊥	Limit of restricted area	⌐ T T T T T T T T
15	— — — — / — — — —	Maritime limit in general	⌐ — — — — —
16	PRECAUTIONARY AREA ⚠	Precautionary area	⚠ Precautionary Area

NOTES

M Tracks, Routes

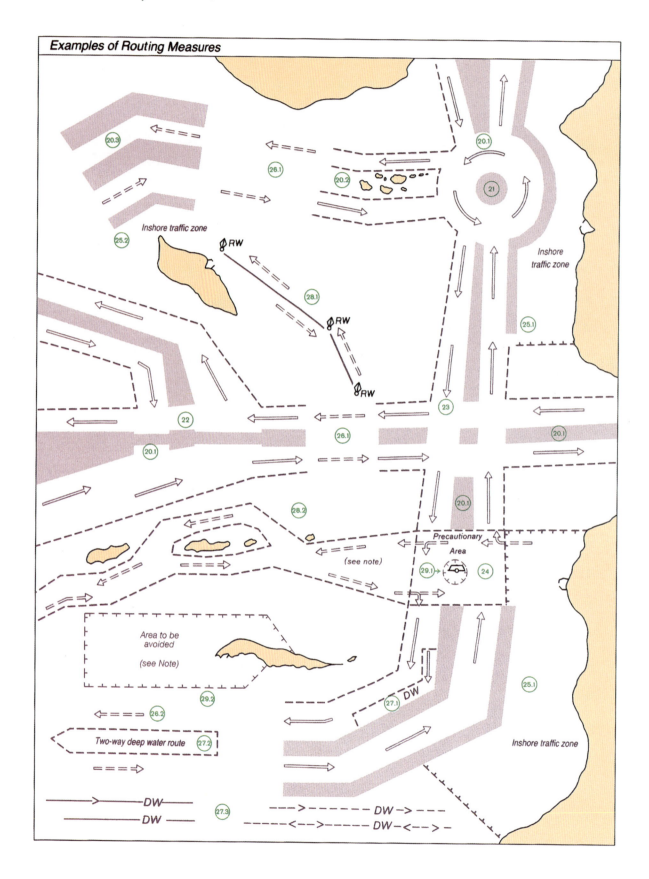

M Tracks, Routes

Examples of Routing Measures

(20.1)	Traffic separation scheme, traffic separated by separation zone
(20.2)	Traffic separation scheme, traffic separated by natural obstructions
(20.3)	Traffic separation scheme, with outer separation zone, separating traffic using scheme from traffic not using it
(21)	Traffic separation scheme, roundabout
(22)	Traffic separation scheme, with "crossing gates"
(23)	Traffic separation schemes crossing, without designated precautionary area
(24)	Precautionary area
(25.1)	Inshore traffic zone, with defined end-limits
(25.2)	Inshore traffic zone without defined end-limits
(26.1)	Recommended direction of traffic flow, between Traffic separation schemes
(26.2)	Recommended direction of traffic flow, for ships not needing a deep water route
(27.1)	Deep water route, as part of one-way traffic lane
(27.2)	Two-way deep water route, with minimum depth stated
(27.3)	Deep water route, centerline as recommended One-way or Two-way track
(28.1)	Recommended route (often marked by centerline buoys)
(28.2)	Two-way route with one-way sections
(29.1)	Area to be avoided, around navigational aid
(29.2)	Area to be avoided, because of danger of stranding

M Tracks, Routes

Radar Surveillance Systems

30	⊙ Ra		Radar Surveillance Station	° Radar Surveillance Station	
31			Radar range	Ra Cuxhaven	
32.1			Radar reference line	------- Ra -------	—Ra——Ra—
32.2			Radar reference line coinciding with a leading line	Ra 270°-090°	

Radio Reporting Points

40	◁A ◁B ◁3		Radio reporting (calling-in or way) points showing direction(s) of vessel movement with designation (if any)	◁A ◁B ◁7

Ferries

50	Ferry	Ferry	------□------
51	Cable ferry	Cable Ferry	------□------ Cable Ferry

Supplementary National Symbols

a	←→DW←→	Recommended track for deep draft vessels (track not defined by fixed marks)	
b	←→DW 83 ft←→ DW 78 ft	Depth is shown where it has been obtained by the cognizant authority	
c	----- -----	Alternate course	
d	(roundabout symbol)	Established traffic separation scheme: Roundabout	
e	○	If no separation zone exists, the center of the roundabout is shown by a circle	

54

N Areas, Limits

| Dredged and Swept Areas → I | Submarine Cables, Submarine Pipelines → L | Tracks, Routes → M |

General

1.1	⌐ ─ ─ ─ ─ ─ ┐	Maritime limit in general usually implying: Permanent obstructions	⌐ ─ ─ ─ ─ ─ ┐
1.2	⌐ ─ ─ ─ ─ ─	Maritime limit in general usually implying: No permanent obstructions	⌐ ─ ─ ─ ─ ─ ┐
2.1	Restricted Area	Limit of restricted area	
2.2	PROHIBITED AREA / PROHIB AREA	(Screen optional) / Limit of prohibited area (no unauthorized entry)	Entry Prohibited

Anchorages, Anchorage Areas

10	⚓ / ⚓ ⚓	⚓ / ⚓	Anchorage (large vessels) / Anchorage (small vessels)	⚓	⚓ ⚓ ⚓
11.1	(14)		Anchor berths	(A)⚓ N53⚓ (14)⚓	(6) No1 ⚓
11.2	(3) green circle	D17	Anchor berths, swinging circle may be shown	(A)⚓ (N53)⚓ (14)⚓ dashed	
12.1	─ ─ ─ ─ ─	⚓ Anchorage	Anchorage area in general	rectangle with ⚓ symbols	
12.2		Anchorage No 1	Numbered anchorage area	No1 ⚓	
12.3		Neufeld Anchorage	Named anchorage area	Neufeld ⚓	
12.4		DW Anchprage	Deep Water Anchorage area, Anchorage area for Deep Draft Vessels	DW ⚓	
12.5		Tanker Anchorage	Tanker anchorage area	Tanker ⚓	

N Areas, Limits

12.6			Anchorage for periods up to 24 hours	24 h ⚓	
12.7	Explosives Anchorage		Explosives anchorage area	⚓ (explosives)	
12.8	QUAR ANCH / QUARANTINE ANCHORAGE	Quarantine Anchorage	Quarantine anchorage area	⊕ ⚓	⚓ (quarantine)
12.9			Reserved anchorage	Reserved ⚓ (see Caution)	Anch Reserved

Note: Anchors as part of the limit symbol are not shown for small areas. Other types of anchorage areas may be shown.

13			Sea-plane landing area		⚓ Y ⚓
14			Anchorage for sea-planes	⚓ (sea-plane)	

Restricted Areas

20	ANCH PROHIB / Anch Prohibited	ANCH PROHIB	Anchoring prohibited		
21	Fish Prohibited	FISH PROHIB	Fishing prohibited		
22	————	┆ ————	Limit of nature reserve: Nature reserve / Bird sanctuary / Game preserve / Seal sanctuary		
23.1	Explosives Dumping Ground	Explosives Dumping Ground	Explosives dumping ground	Explosives Dumping Ground	
23.2	Explosives Dumping Ground (Discontd)	Explosives Dumping Ground (disused)	Explosives dumping ground (disused) Foul (explosives)	Explosives Dumping Ground (disused)	

N Areas, Limits

24	Dump Site	Dumping Ground	Dumping ground for chemical waste	Dumping Ground for Chemical waste	
25	Degaussing Range	Degaussing Range	Degaussing range	Degaussing range	
26		Historic Wreck (see note)	Historic wreck and restricted area	Historic Wk	

Military Practice Areas					
30			Firing danger area		
31	PROHIBITED AREA	Prohibited Area	Military area, entry prohibited	Entry Prohibited	
32			Mine-laying practice area		
33			Submarine transit lane and exercise area		
34			Mine field	Minefield (see Caution)	

International Boundaries and National Limits				Supplementary national symbols: a, b	
40	++++++++	— — —	International boundary on land	DENMARK ++++++++ FEDERAL REPUBLIC OF GERMANY	
41	CANADA / UNITED STATES	—+—+—+—	International maritime boundary	DENMARK / FEDERAL REPUBLIC OF GERMANY	
42		— — —	Straight territorial sea baseline		
43		—+—+—	Seaward limit of territorial sea	—+—+—	
44		—+—	Seaward limit of contiguous zone	—+—	

57

N Areas, Limits

45	—◇—		Limits of fishery zones	—————◇———— — — — ◇ — — —	
46			Limit of continental shelf		
47	—◇—		Limit of Exclusive Economic Zone	———— EEZ ————	
48			Customs limit	— — — ⊖ — — —	— — — — —
49		Harbor Limit	Harbor limit	Harbour limit	— · — · —

Various Limits

Supplementary national symbols: c-g

60.1			Limit of fast ice, Ice front	⋎⋎⋎⋎⋎⋎	
60.2			Limit of sea ice (pack ice)-seasonal	⋎⋎⋎⋎⋎⋎	
61	Log boom		Log pond	Log Pond	ǀ — ǀ — ǀ —
62.1	Spoil Area		Spoil ground	Spoil Ground	⌐∿⌐
62.2	Spoil Area Discontinued		Spoil ground (disused)	Spoil Ground (disused)	
63			Dredging area	Dredging Area (see Note)	
64			Cargo transhipment area	Cargo Transhipment Area	
65			Incineration area	Incineration Area	

Supplementary National Symbols

a	— — — — —		COLREGS demarcation line
b	— — —		Limit of fishing areas (fish trap areas)
c	Dumping Ground		Dumping ground

N Areas, Limits

d	Disposal Area 92 depths from survey of JUNE 1972 85	Disposal area (Dump Site)	
e	------------------	Limit of airport	
f	— · — · — ▬▬▬	Reservation line (Options)	
g	┌ ─ ─ ─ ─ ┐ │ Dump Site │ └	Dump site	

O Hydrographic Terms

1		Ocean
2		Sea
3	G	Gulf
4	B	Bay, Bayou
5	Fd	Fjord
6	L	Loch, Lough, Lake
7	Cr	Creek
8	Lag	Lagoon
9	C	Cove
10	In	Inlet
11	Str	Strait
12	Sd	Sound
13	Pass	Passage, Pass
14	Chan	Channel
15		Narrows
16	Entr	Entrance
17	Est	Estuary
18		Delta
19	Mth	Mouth
20	Rd	Roads, Roadstead
21	Anch	Anchorage
22	Apprs	Approach, Approaches
23	Bk	Bank
24		
25	Shl	Shoal
26	Rf Co rf	Reef, Coral reef
27		Sunken rock
28	Le	Ledge
29		Pinnacle
30		Ridge
31		Rise
32	Mt	Mountain, Mount
33		Seamount
34		Seamount chain
35	Pk	Peak
36		Knoll
37		Abyssal hill
38		Tablemount
39		Plateau
40		Terrace
41		Spur
42		Continental shelf

43		Shelf-edge
44		Slope
45		Continental slope
46		Continental rise
47		Continental borderland
48		Basin
49		Abyssal plain
50		Hole
51		Trench
52		Trough
53		Valley
54		Median Valley
55		Canyon
56		Seachannel
57		Moat, Sea moat
58		Fan
59		Apron
60		Fracture zone
61		Scarp, Escarpment
62		Sill
63		Gap
64		Saddle
65		Levee
66		Province
67		Tideway, Tidal gully
68		Sidearm

Other Terms

80		projected
81		lighted
82		buoyed
83		marked
84	anc	ancient
85	dist	distant
86		lesser
87		closed
88		partly
89	approx	approximate
90	Subm, subm	submerged
91		shoaled
92	exper	experimental
93	D, Destr	destroyed

P Lights

\multicolumn{7}{l}{Light Structures, Major Floating Lights}

1	ᵒ !			Major light, minor light light, lighthouse	! ☆ ! ★ Lt Lt Ho	✦ ● ★ ·
2	■ PLATFORM (lighted)		▫!	Lighted offshore platform	▫!	
3	○ Marker (lighted)	!BY	!	Lighted beacon tower	!BY ☆ Bn Tr	
4		▫!R	!	Lighted beacon	▫!R •!BRB ☆ Bn	
5	○ Art	▫!R	!	Articulated light Buoyant beacon, résilient beacon	!R ☆ Bn	
6		⚓!		Light vessel; Lightship Normally manned light-vessel	⚓!	⚓!
7		⚓!		Unmanned light-vessel; light float		!FLOAT
8	⟂!			LANBY, superbuoy as navigational aid		

61

P Lights

Light Characters

Light Characters on Light Buoys → Q

	Abbreviation International	Abbreviation National	Class of light	Illustration / Period shown	
10.1	F	F	Fixed		F
10.2	\[Occulting (total duration of light longer than total duration of darkness)\]				
	Oc	Oc	Single-occulting		Oc
	Oc(2) Example	Oc (2)	Group-occulting		Oc (2)
	Oc(2+3) Example	Oc(2+3)	Composite group-occulting		Oc(2+3)
10.3	\[Isophase (duration of light and darkness equal)\]				
	Iso	Iso	Isophase		Iso
10.4	\[Flashing (total duration of light shorter than total duration of darkness)\]				
	Fl	Fl	Single-flashing		Fl
	Fl(3) Example	Fl (3)	Group-flashing		Fl (3)
	Fl(2+1) Example	Fl (2+1)	Composite group-flashing		Fl (2+1)
10.5	LFl	L Fl	Long-flashing (flash 2 s or longer)		L Fl
10.6	\[Quick (repetition rate of 50 to 79 – usually either 50 or 60 – flashes per minute)\]				
	Q	Q	Continuous quick		Q
	Q(3) Example	Q(3)	Group quick		
	IQ	IQ	Interrupted quick		IQ

P Lights

	Abbreviation		Class of light	Illustration	Period shown ⊢——⊣	
	International	National				
	Very quick (repetition rate of 80 to 159 – usually either 100 or 120 – flashes per min)					
10.7	VQ	VQ	Continuous very quick			VQ
	VQ(3) Example	VQ (3)	Group very quick			
	IVQ	IVQ	Interrupted very quick			
	Ultra quick (repetition rate of 160 or more – usually 240 to 300 – flashes per min)					
10.8	UQ	UQ	Continuous ultra quick			
	IUQ	IUQ	Interrupted ultra quick			
10.9	Mo (A) Example	Mo (A)	Morse Code			
10.10	FFl	F Fl	Fixed and flashing			F Fl
10.11	Al.WR	AlWR	Alternating			AlWR

Colors of Lights

11.1	W		W		White (only on sector- and alternating lights)
11.2	R		R		Red
11.3	G		G		Green
11.4	Bu		Bu		Blue
11.5	Vi		Vi		Violet
11.6	Y		Y		Yellow
11.7	Y	Or	Y	Or	Orange
11.8	Y	Am	Y	Am	Amber

Colors of lights shown on standard charts

on multicolored charts

on multicolored charts at sector lights

P Lights

Period				
12	90s		Period in seconds	90s
Elevation				
Plane of Reference for Heights → H				Tidal Levels → H
13	12m 36ft		Elevation of light given in meters or feet	12m
Range				
Note: Charted ranges are nominal ranges given in Nautical miles				
14	15M	15M	Light with single range	15M
	10M	15/10M	Light with two different ranges NOS: only lesser of two ranges is charted	15/10M
	7M	15-7M	Light with three or more ranges NOS: only least of three ranges is charted	15-7M
Disposition				
15		(hor)	horizontally disposed	(hor)
		(vert)	vertically disposed	(vert)

Example of a full Light Description

16		Name Fl (3) WRG 15s 21ft 11M Fl (3) WRG 15s 21m 15-11M-NIMA		Name Fl(3)WRG.15s 21m 15-11M	
	Fl(3)	Class of light: group flashing repeating a group of three flashes	Fl(3)	Class of light: group flashing repeating a group of three flashes	
	WRG	Colors: white, red, green, exhibiting the different colors in defined sectors	WRG	Colors: white, red, green, exhibiting the different colors in defined sectors	
	15s	Period: the time taken to exhibit one full sequence of 3 flashes and eclipses: 15 seconds	15s	Period: the time taken to exhibit one full sequence of 3 flashes and eclipses: 15 seconds	
	21ft } 21m }	Elevation of focal plane above datum: 21 feet or 21 meters	21m	Elevation of focal plane above datum: 21 meters	
	11M } 15-11M }	Nominal range NIMA: white 15M, green 11M, red between 15 and 11M.	15-11M	Nominal range: white 15 M, green 11 M, red between 15 and 11 M	

64

P Lights

Lights Marking Fairways			
Leading Lights and Lights in Line			
20.1	Lts in line 270°	Leading lights with leading line (firm line is fairway) and arcs of visibility Bearing given in degrees and tenths of a degree	Name Oc.3s 8m 12M Name Oc.6s 24m 15M
20.2		Leading lights ‡: any two objects in line Bearing given in degrees and minutes	Oc.4s 12M Oc.R 4s 10M Oc.R & Oc ≠ 269°18'
20.3	F Bu, Iso 2s	Leading lights on small-scale charts	Ldg Oc.R & F.R
21		Lights in line, marking the sides of a channel	Fl.G / Fl.G 270° 2 Fl.R 270°
22		Rear or upper light	Rear Lt or Upper Lt
23		Front or lower light	Front Lt or Lower Lt
Direction Lights			
30.1	RED / GREEN	Direction light with narrow sector and course to be followed, flanked by darkness or unintensified light	Dir 269° Fl(2) 5s 10m 11M
30.2		Direction light with course to be followed, uncharted sector is flanked by darkness or unintensified light	Oc.12s 6M Dir 299° Dir 255.5° Fl(2) 5s 11M
30.3		Direction light with narrow fairway sector flanked by sectors of different character	F.G / Al.WR / Oc.W.4s / Al.WR / F.R Dir WRG. 15-5M
31		Moiré effect light (day and night) Arrows show when course alteration needed	Dir 295°
Note: Quoted bearings are always from seaward.			

P Lights

	Sector Lights		
40		Sector light on standard charts	Fl.WRG.4s 21m 18-12M
41.1		Sector lights on standard charts, the white sector limits marking the sides of the fairway	Oc.WRG. 10-6M
41.2		Sector lights on multicoloured charts, the white sector limits marking the sides of the fairway	Oc.WRG. 10-6M
42		Main light visible all-round with red subsidiary light seen over danger	Fl(3) 10s 62m 25M F.R.55m 12M
43		All-round light with obscured sector	Fl.5s 41m 30M
44		Light with arc of visibility deliberately restricted	Iso.WRG
45		Light with faint sector	Q.14m 5M
46		Light with intensified sector	Oc.R.8s 7M / Oc.R.8s

66

P Lights

	Lights with limited Times of Exhibition				
50	Occas	! F R (occas)	Lights exhibited only when specially needed (for fishing vessels, ferries) and some private lights	☆ F.R. (occas)	
51		! F Bu 9m 6M (F by day)	Daytime light (charted only where the character shown by day differs from that shown at night)	Fl.10s 40m 27M ☆ (F.37m 11M Day)	
52			Fog light (exhibited only in fog, or character changes in fog)	Name ☆ Q.WRG.5m 10-3M Fl.5S (in fog)	
53			Unwatched (unmanned) light with no standby or emergency arrangements	☆ Fl.5s (U)	
54			Temporary	(temp)	
55			Extinguished	(exting)	

	Special Lights				
	Flare Stack (at Sea) → L		Flare Stack (on Land) → E		Signal Stations → T
60	! AERO	! AERO Al WG 7½s 108m 13M	Aero light	✣ Aero Al.Fl.WG.7.5s 11M	★ AERO
61.1		! AERO F R 77m 11M	Air obstruction light of high intensity	Aero F.R.313m 11M ✣ RADIO MAST (353)	
61.2		⊙ TR (R Lts)	Air obstruction lights of low intensity	(89) ↑ (R Lts)	
62		Fog Det Lt	Fog detector light	Fog Det Lt	
63		🔦	Floodlight, floodlighting of a structure	🔦 (Illuminated)	
64			Strip light		
65	! Priv	! F R (priv)	Private light other than one exhibited occasionally	! F.R.(priv)	★ ● Priv maintd

	Supplementary National Symbols				
a	🌸		Riprap surrounding light		
b			Short-Long Flashing		S-L Fl
c			Group-Short Flashing		ᴧᴧᴧ ᴧᴧᴧ ᴧᴧᴧ
d			Fixed and Group Flashing		F Gp Fl

Q Buoys, Beacons

Buoys and Beacons					
IALA Maritime Buoyage System, which includes Beacons → Q 130					
1	○	–○–	Position of buoy		–○–
Colors of Buoys and Beacon Topmarks					
Abbreviations for Colors → P					
2			Green and black		
3			Single colors other than green and black		
4			Multiple colors in horizontal bands, the color sequence is from top to bottom		
5			Multiple colors in vertical or diagonal stripes, the darker color is given first		
6			Retroreflecting material		

Note: Retroreflecting material may be fitted to some unlit marks. Charts do not usually show it. Under IALA Recommendations, black bands will appear blue under a spotlight.

Lighted Marks					
Marks with Fog Signals → R					
7		Fl.R Fl.G	Lighted marks on standard charts		Fl.G Fl.R
8			Lighted marks on multicolored charts		Fl.R Iso Fl.G
Topmarks and Radar Reflectors					
For Application of Topmarks within the IALA-System → Q 130 Topmarks on Special Purpose Buoys and Beacons → Q					
9			IALA System buoy topmarks (beacon topmarks shown upright)		
10		No 2	Beacon with topmark, color, radar reflector and designation		No 2 Name
11		No 3	Buoy with topmark, color, radar reflector and designation		No 3

Note: Radar reflectors on floating marks are usually not charted.

Q Buoys, Beacons

Buoys	Features Common to Buoys and Beacons → Q 1–11				
Shapes of Buoys					
20	⚲ N △	△	Conical buoy, nun buoy	△	
21	⚲ C ⌑	⌑	Can or cylindrical buoy	⌑	
22	⚲ SP ◠	◠	Spherical buoy	◠	
23	⚲ P ⚑	⚑	Pillar buoy	⚑	
24	⚲ S ⎸	⎸	Spar buoy, spindle buoy	⎸	
25	⚲ ⌒	⌒	Barrel buoy	⌒	
26	⚓	⚓	Super buoy	⚓	
Light Floats					
30	⚐	Fl G 3s Name	Light float as part of IALA System	Fl.G.3s No 3 Name	⚐
31		Fl(2) 10s 11M	Light float (unmanned light-vessel) not part of IALA System	Fl.10s 12m 26M	
Mooring Buoys					
Oil or Gas Installation Buoy → L				Small Craft Mooring → U	
40	⚓		Mooring buoys	△ ◒ ⌑ ⚑	
41	⚓	Fl Y 2s	Lighted mooring buoy (example)	Fl.Y.2.5s	
42			Trot, mooring buoys with ground tackle and berth numbers	(diagram with berths ① ②)	
43	See Supplementary national symbols m, n		Mooring buoy with telegraphic or telephonic communication	⚓〜〜〜〜〜	

44		⚓ (5 buoys) Moorings	Numerous moorings (example)	⌐ ─ ─ ─ ─ ┐
				  Small Craft
				  Moorings
				└ ─ ─ ─ ─ ┘	

Q Buoys, Beacons

	Special Purpose Buoys		
	*Note: Shapes of buoys are variable. Lateral or Cardinal buoys may be used in some situations.*		
50		Firing danger area (Danger Zone) buoy	DZ
51		Target	Target
52		Marker Ship	Marker Ship
53		Barge	Barge
54		Degaussing Range buoy	
55	Tel	Cable buoy	
56		Spoil ground buoy	
57		Buoy marking outfall	
58	ODAS / W or, special-purpose buoys	ODAS-buoy (Ocean-Data-Acquisition System). Data-Collecting buoy of superbuoy size / Special-purpose buoys	ODAS
59		Wave recorder, current meter	
60	AERO	Seaplane anchorage buoy	
61		Buoy marking traffic separation scheme	
62		Buoy marking recreation zone	
	Seasonal Buoys		
70	Priv (maintained by private interests, use with caution)	Buoy privately maintained (example)	(priv)
71		Seasonal buoy (example)	(Apr – Oct)

Q Buoys, Beacons

Beacons					
Lighted Beacons → P			Features Common to Beacons and Buoys → Q 1–11		
80	▢ Bn	⊥ ⊙ Bn	Beacon in general. characteristics unknown or chart scale too small to show	⊥ ⊙ Bn	
81	▢ RW ▲ ▪	⊥ BW	Beacon with color. no distinctive topmark	⊥ BW	
82		⊥ R ⊥ BY	Beacons with colors and topmarks (examples)	⊥ R ⊥ BY ⊥ BRB	
83			Beacon on submerged rock (topmark as appropriate)	⊥ BRB	⟋ BRB

Minor impermanent Marks usually in drying Areas (Lateral Mark of Minor Channel)					
Minor Pile → F					
90	∘ Pole • Pole	⊥	Stake. pole	⊥	
91	∘ Stake • Stake	⊥	Perch. stake	PORT HAND Y	STARBOARD HAND ↑
92			Withy	⌇	⌇

Minor Marks, usually on Land					
Landmarks → E					
100	⊙ CAIRN ∘ Cairn	⊙ CAIRN ∘ Cairn	Cairn	⩎	
101			Colored or white mark	▢ Mk	

Beacon Towers					
110	▢ RW	♨ R ♨ G ♨ R ♨ G	Beacon towers without and with topmarks and colors (examples)	♨ R ♨ G ♨ R ♨ G ♨ BY ♨ BRB	
111			Lattice beacon	♨	

Q Buoys, Beacons

Special Purpose Beacons					
Leading Lines, Clearing Lines → M					
Note: Topmarks and colors shown where scale permits.					
120	(diagram: Bns in line 270°)		Leading beacons	(diagram)
121		(diagram: Bns in line 270°)	Beacons marking a clearing line	(diagram)
122	(diagram: COURSE 270°00' TRUE, MARKERS)		Beacons marking measured distance with quoted bearings	(diagram: Measured Distance 1852m 090°- 270)
123		(diagram: W)	Cable landing beacon (example)	(diagram: Y)
124			Refuge beacon	Ref. Ref.
125			Firing danger area beacons	
126		(symbol)	Notice board	(symbol)

72

Q Buoys, Beacons

130 IALA Maritime Buoyage System
IALA International Association of Lighthouse Authorities
Where in force, the IALA System applies to all fixed and floating marks except lighthouses, sector lights, leading lights and leading marks, light-vessels and lanbys. The standard buoy shapes are cylindrical (can), conical, spherical, pillar, and spar, but variations may occur, for example: light-floats. In the illustrations below, only the standard buoy shapes are used. In the case of fixed beacons (lit or unlit) only the shape of the topmark is of navigational significance.

130.1 *Lateral marks* are generally for well-defined channels. There are two international Buoyage Regions – A and B – where Lateral marks differ.

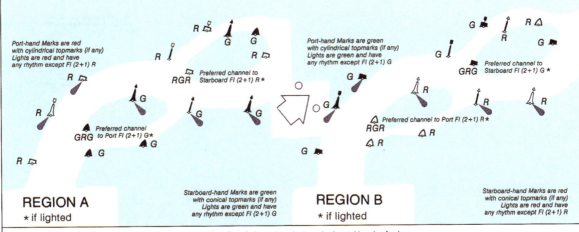

REGION A
* if lighted

Port-hand Marks are red with cylindrical topmarks (if any) Lights are red and have any rhythm except Fl (2+1) R

Starboard-hand Marks are green with conical topmarks (if any) Lights are green and have any rhythm except Fl (2+1) G

REGION B
* if lighted

Port-hand Marks are green with cylindrical topmarks (if any) Lights are green and have any rhythm except Fl (2+1) G

Starboard-hand Marks are red with conical topmarks (if any) Lights are red and have any rhythm except Fl (2+1) R

A preferred channel buoy may also be a pillar or a spar. All preferred channel marks have horizontal bands of color.
Where for exceptional reasons an Authority considers that a green color for buoys is not satisfactory, black may be used.

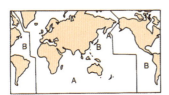

IALA Buoyage Regions A and B

130.2 *Direction of Buoyage*
The direction of buoyage is that taken when approaching a harbor from seaward or along coasts, the direction determined by buoyage authorities, normally clockwise around land masses.

 Symbol showing direction of buoyage where not obvious.

 Symbol showing direction of buoyage on multicolored charts.

Q Buoys, Beacons

In the illustrations below all marks are the same in Regions A and B.

130.3 Cardinal Marks indicating navigable water to the named side of the marks.

UNLIT MARKS

Topmark: 2 black cones

- North Mark — Black above yellow
- East Mark — Black with yellow band
- South Mark — Yellow above black
- West Mark — Yellow with black band

LIGHTED MARKS

White Light — Time (seconds) 0 5 10 15

Mark	Symbol	Light
North Mark	N BY	VQ or Q
East Mark	E BYB	VQ(3)5s or Q(3)10s
South Mark	S YB	VQ(6)+LFl 10s or Q(6)+LFl 15s
West Mark	W YBY	VQ(9)10s or Q(9)15s

The same abbreviations are used for lights on spar buoys and beacons. The periods 5s, 10s and 15s, may not always be charted.

130.4 Isolated Danger Marks stationed over dangers with navigable water around them.

Body: black with red horizontal band(s)
Topmark: 2 black spheres

BRB   BRB   BRB   BRB   Fl(2)   white light

130.5 Safe Water Marks such as mid-channel and landfall marks.

Body: red and white vertical stripes
Topmark (if any): red sphere

RW   RW   RW   RW   RW   Oc, or Iso, or L Fl 10s, or Mo (A)   white light

130.6 Special Marks not primarily to assist navigation but to indicate special features.

Body (shape optional): yellow ‡
Topmark (if any): yellow ✕

Y   Y   Y   Y   Y   Fl.Y etc.   yellow light (rhythm optional)

‡ In special cases yellow can be in conjunction with another color.

BEACONS with IALA System topmarks are charted by upright symbols, eg. BYB, BRB (minor beacon) or, on smaller-scale charts: Bn R, Bn G

Beacon towers are charted: R, G, BRB etc. (occasionally lighted)

RADAR REFLECTORS on buoys and beacons are not generally charted.

COLOR ABBREVIATIONS under symbols, especially those of spar buoys, may be omitted, or may be at variance with symbols shown above.

LIGHT FLOATS: The IALA System is not usually applied to large lightfloats (replacing manned lightships) but may be applied to smaller lightfloats.

Q Buoys, Beacons

	Supplementary National Symbols			
a	♂BELL ⚐BELL		Bell buoy	
b	♂GONG ⚐GONG		Gong buoy	
c	♂WHIS ⚐WHIS		Whistle buoy	
d	♂RW		Fairway buoy (RWVS)	
e	♂RW		Midchannel buoy (RWVS)	
f	♂R "2"		Starboard - hand buoy (entering from seaward - US waters)	
g	♂"1" ♂"1"		Port - hand buoy (entering from seaward - US waters)	
h	♂BR ♂RG ♂GR ♂G		Bifurcation, Junction, Isolated danger, Wreck and Obstruction buoys	
i	♂Y		Fish trap (area) buoy	
j	♂Y		Anchorage buoy (marks limits)	
k	B		Black	
l	△R Bn △RG Bn		Triangular shaped beacons	
	■G Bn □GR Bn □W Bn □B Bn		Square shaped beacons	
	□Bn		Beacon, color unknown	
m		⛵Tel ⚓Tel	Mooring buoy with telegraphic communications	
n		⛵T ⚓T	Mooring buoy with telephonic communications	
o	⚐		Lighted beacon	!Bn ⚐

75

R Fog Signals

General

	Fog Detector Light → P			Fog Light → P
1	Fog Sig)))	)))	Position of fog signal. Type of fog signal not stated	[symbols] etc.

Types of Fog Signals, with Abbreviations

Supplementary national symbols: a

10	GUN	Explosive	Explos
11	DIA	Diaphone	Dia
12	SIREN	Siren	Siren
13	HORN	Horn (nautophone, reed, tyfon)	Horn
14	BELL	Bell	Bell
15	WHIS	Whistle	Whis
16	GONG	Gong	Gong

Examples of Fog Signal Descriptions

20	Fl 3s 70m 29M SIREN Mo(N) 60s	Fl 3s 70m 29M SIREN	Siren at a lighthouse, giving a long blast followed by a short one (N), repeated every 60 seconds	Fl.3s 70m 29M Siren Mo(N)60S ‡
21	BELL	BELL	Wave-actuated bell buoy	Bell ‡
22	Q(6)+LFl 15s HORN(1) 15s WHIS	Q(6)+LFl 15s YB HORN WHIS	Light buoy, with horn giving a single blast every 15 seconds, in conjunction with a wave-actuated whistle	Q(6)+LFl.15s YB Horn(1) 15s Whis ‡
	‡ The fog signal symbol may be omitted when a description of the signal is given.			

R   Fog Signals

Supplementary National Symbols				
a	Mo		Morse Code fog signal	

S Radar, Radio, Electronic Position-Fixing Systems

Radar

Radar Structures Forming Landmarks → E   *Radar Surveillance Systems → M*

1	Ra	Coast radar station, providing range and bearing service on request		Ra
2	Ramark	Ramark, radar beacon transmitting continuously		Ramark
3.1	RACON	Radar transponder beacon, with morse identification, responding within the 3-cm(X-)band		Racon(Z)
3.2		Radar transponder beacon, with morse identification, responding within the 10-cm(S-)band		Racon(Z) (10cm)
3.3		Radar transponder beacon, responding within the 3-cm(X-) and the 10-cm(S-)band		Racon(Z) (3&10cm)
3.4		Radar transponder beacon, responding on a fixed frequency outside the marine band		F Racon
3.5		Radar transponder beacons with bearing line		Racons ≠ 270° Racon Racon
3.6	RACON (−) R "2" Fl R 4s	Racon	Floating marks with radar transponder beacons	Racon Racon
4	Ra Ref		Radar reflector	
5	Ra (conspic)		Radar-conspicuous feature	

Radio

Radio Structures Forming Landmarks → E   *Radio Reporting (Calling-in or Way) Points → M*

10	R Bn, RC	Circular (non-directional) marine or aeromarine radiobeacon	Name RC
11	RD 072°30′ RD	Directional radiobeacon with bearing line	RD RD 269.5°
12	RW	Rotating-pattern radiobeacon	RW

S *Radar, Radio, Electronic Position-Fixing Systems*

13	⊙ CONSOL Bn 190 kHz MMF ▄▄.	⊙ CONSOL	Consol beacon	⊙ Consol
14	⊙ RDF		Radio direction-finding station	⊙ RG
15	∘ R Sta	⊙ R	Coast radio station providing QTG service	⊙ R
16	⊙ AERO R Bn		Aeronautical radiobeacon	⊙ Aero R C

Electronic Position-Fixing Systems

Decca

20	AB AC AD	Identification of Lattice Patterns	AB AC AD
21	————	Line of Position (LOP)	————
22	————	Line of Position representing Zone Limit (or, on larger scales) other intermediate LOPs	————
23	— — —	Half-lane LOP	— — —
24	— — — —	LOP from adjoining Chain (on Interchain Fixing Charts)	— — — —
25	A 12	Lane value, with Chain designator (Interchain charts only) and Zone designator	(6) A 12

Note: A Decca Chain Coverage Diagram is given when patterns from more than one Chain appear on a chart. LOPs are normally theoretical ones: if Fixed Error is included, an explanatory note is given.

Loran-C

30	9960-Y 9960-Z	Identification of Loran-C-Rates	7970-X
31	————	Line of Position (LOP)	————
32	————	LOP representing time difference value of an integral thousand µs (microseconds)	————
33		LOP beyond reliable groundwave service area	— — —

S *Radar, Radio, Electronic Position-Fixing Systems*

34		LOP from adjoining Chain		─ ─ ─ ─ ─ ─ ─
35		LOP from adjoining Chain beyond reliable groundwave service area		─ ─ ─ ─ ─ ─ ─
36	9960-Z-58000	LOP labelled with rate and full us value		7970-X 33000
37		050	LOP labelled with final three digits only		050

Note: A Loran-C Chain Diagram may be given if rates from more than one Chain appear on a chart. An explanatory note is given if LOPs include propagation delays.

Omega

40	DF CF AC	Charted station pairs	AB BC
41	────────	Line of Position (LOP)	────────
42	DF - 702	Lane values	897 AB-900

Note: A cautionary note draws attention to the need to consult Propagation Prediction Correction (PPC) tables. An explanatory note draws attention to the unreliability of LOPs within 450 n miles of a transmitter.

Satellite Navigation Systems

50	WGS WGS 72 WGS 84	World Geodetic System. 1972 or 1984	WGS WGS 72 WGS 84

Note: A note may be shown to indicate the shifts of latitude and longitude. in hundredths of a minute, which should be made to satellite-derived positions (which are referred to WGS) to relate them to the chart.

T Services

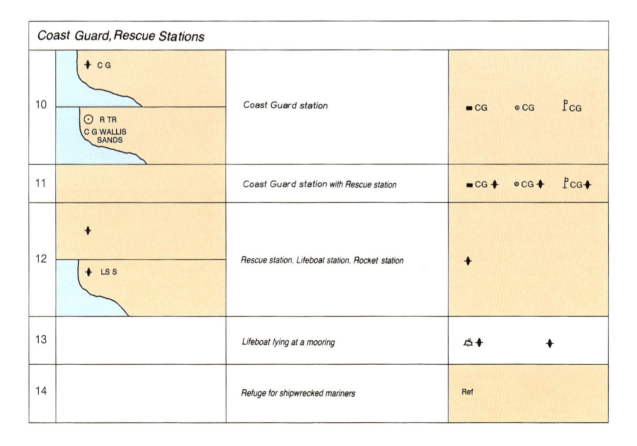

T Services

Signal Stations

20	⊙ S S		Signal station in general	⊙ SS	⚲ Sig Sta
21			Signal station, showing International Port Traffic Signals	⊙ SS (INT)	
22			Traffic signal station, Port entry and Departure signals	⊙ SS (Traffic)	
23	○ HECP		Port control signal station	⊙ SS (Port control)	
24			Lock signal station	⊙ SS (Lock)	
25.1			Bridge passage signal station	⊙ SS (Bridge)	
25.2			Bridge lights including traffic signals	F Traffic-Sig	
26			Distress signal station	⊙ SS	
27			Telegraph station	⊙ SS	
28	S Sig Sta		Storm signal station	⊙ SS (Storm)	
29	⊙ NWS SIG STA		National Weather Service signal station, Wind signal station	⊙ SS (Weather)	
30			Ice signal station	⊙ SS (Ice)	
31			Time signal station	⊙ SS (Time)	
32.1		○ Tide gauge	Tide scale or gauge	‡	
32.2			Automatically recording tide gauge	⊙ Tide gauge	
33			Tidal signal station	⊙ SS (Tide)	
34			Tidal stream signal	⊙ SS (Stream)	
35			Danger signal station	⊙ SS (Danger)	
36			Firing practice signal station	⊙ SS (Firing)	

Supplementary National Symbols

a	○ BELL		Bell (on land)	
b				
c	○ MARINE POLICE		Marine police station	
d	○ FIREBOAT STATION		Fireboat station	
e	⚇		Notice board	
f	⊙ LOOK TR		Lookout station; Watch tower	
g	Sem		Semaphore	
h	◓		Park Ranger station	

U *Small Craft Facilities*

Small Craft Facilities		
Traffic Features, Bridges → D	*Public Buildings, Cranes → F*	*Pilots, Coastguard, Rescue, Signal Stations → T*
1.1	Boat harbor, Marina	⚓
1.2	Yacht berths without facilities	
2	Visitors' berth	
3	Visitors' mooring	
4	Yacht club, Sailing club	
5	Slipway	
6	Boat hoist	
7	Public landing, Steps, Ladder	
8	Sailmaker	
9	Boatyard	
10	Public inn	
11	Restaurant	
12	Chandler	
13	Provisions	
14	Bank, Exchange office	
15	Physician, Doctor	
16	Pharmacy, Chemist	
17	Water tap	
18	Fuel station (Petrol, Diesel)	
19	Electricity	

U *Small Craft Facilities*

20		Bottle gas	
21		Showers	
22		Laundrette	
23		Public toilets	
24		Post box	
25		Public telephone	
26		Refuse bin	
27		Car park	
28		Parking for boats and trailers	
29		Caravan site	
30	⋀	Camping site	
31		Water Police	

Marina facilities

32

No	LOCATION	APPROACH - FEET (REPORTED)	ALONGSIDE - FEET (REPORTED)	ELECTRICITY (TRANSIENTS)	RAMP - SURFACED - NATURAL	REPAIRS - HULL - MOTOR - RADIO	MOORINGS - BERTHS	MARINE RAILWAY - FEET	LIFT CAPACITY - TONS	BOAT RENTAL CANOE - ROW - MOTOR	CHARTER - HOUSE - SAIL	FOOD - LODGING - CAMPING	TOILETS - SHOWERS - LAUNDRY	PUMP - OUT STATION	WINTER STORAGE WET - DRY	WATER - ICE	NAUTICAL CHART - SALES	GROCERIES	BAIT - TACKLE	DIESEL OIL - GASOLINE	HARDWARE
1	LAS VEGAS BOAT							80	20		S	HM		M		F C	T	P	WD	C	W I	GH	BT	G
2	LAKE MEAD MAR				B E			80	15		S	HM		M		FL	T	P	WD	C	W I			DG
3	HEMENWAY HARBOR							80			S													
4	TEMPLE BAR HAR							80	15		SN			M	H	FLC	TSL P	WD	C	W I	GH	BT	G
5	ECHO BAY RESORT							35	35	BM	S	M		M	H	FLC	TSL P	WD	C	W I	GH	BT	G
6	OVERTON BEACH							100			S			M		F C	TSL	WD		W I	G	BT	G
7	CALLVILLE BAY M							100	40		S			M	H	F C	TS P	WD		W I	G	B	G

(+) DENOTES HOURS LATER   (-) DENOTES HOURS EARLIER
THE LOCATIONS OF THE ABOVE PUBLIC MARINE FACILITIES ARE SHOWN ON THE CHART BY LARGE PURPLE NUMBERS.
THE TABULATED "APPROACH - FEET (REPORTED)" IS THE DEPTH AVAILABLE FROM THE NEAREST NATURAL OR DREDGED CHANNEL TO THE FACILITY.
THE TABULATED "PUMPING STATION" IS DEFINED AS FACILITIES AVAILABLE FOR PUMPING OUT BOAT HOLDING TANKS.
(H) APPROACH DEPTH FLUCTUATES WITH LAKE LEVELS.

V Index of Abbreviations

AERO, Aero	Aero light	P 60
AERO RBn	Aeronautical radiobeacon	S 16
Aero RC	Aeronautical radiobeacon	S 16
Al	Alternating	P 10.11
ALP	Articulated Loading Platform	L 12
Alt	Alternating	P 10.11
Am	Amber	P 11.8
anc	Ancient	O 84
ANCH, Anch	Anchorage	N 20, O 21
approx	Approximate	O 90
Apprs	Approaches	O 22
B	Bay, bayou	O 4
Bdy Mon	Boundary monument	B 24
bk	Broken	J 33
Bkw	Breakwater	F 4.1
Bl	Blue	P 11.4
BM	Bench mark	B 23
Bn	Beacon	O 4
Bn Tr	Beacon tower	O 3
Br	Breakers	K 17
brg	Bearing	B 62
brk	Broken	J 33
Bu	Blue	P 11.4
c	Course	J 32
C	Can, cylindrical	Q 21
C	Cove	O 9
CALM	Centenary Anchor Leg Mooring	L 16
Cas	Castle	E 34.2
Cb	Cobbles	J 8
cbl	Cable	B 46
cd	Candela	B 54
CD	Chart datum	H 1
Cem	Cemetery	E 19
CG	Coast Guard station	T 10
Chan	Channel	O 14
Ch.	Church	E 10.1
Chy	Chimney	E 22
Cl	Clay	J 3
CL	Clearance	D 20, D 21
cm	Centimeter(s)	B 43
Co	Coral	J 10
Co rf	Coral reef	O 26
Cr	Creek	O 7
crs	Course	J 32

Cup, Cup.	Cupola	E 10.4
Cus Ho	Customs house	F 61
Cy	Clay	J 3
D	Destroyed	O 94
Destr	Destroyed	O 94
dev	Deviation	B 67
DIA, Dia	Diaphone	R 11
Dir	Direction	P 30, P 31
dist	Distant	O 85
dm	Decimeter(s)	B 42
Dn.	Dolphin	F 20
Dol	Dolphin	F 20
DW	Deep Water route	M 27.1, N 12.4
DZ	Danger Zone	Q 50
E	East, eastern	B 10
ED	Existence doubtful	I 1
EEZ	Exclusive Economic Zone	N 47
E Int	Equal interval, isophase	P 10.3
Entr	Entrance	O 16
Est	Estuary	O 17
exper	Experimental	O 93
Explos	Explosive	R 10
Exting, exting	Extinguished	P 55
f	Fine	J 30
F	Fixed	P 10.1
Fd	Fjord	O 5
F Fl	Fixed and flashing	P 10.10
FISH	Fishing	N 21
Fl	Flashing	P 10.4
Fla	Flare stack	L 11
fm	Fathom	B 48
fms	Fathoms	B 48
fne	Fine	J 30
Fog Det Lt	Fog detector light	P 62
Fog Sig	Fog signal	R 1
FP	Flagpole	E 27
FS, FS.	Flagstaff	E 27
ft	Foot, feet	B 47
G	Gravel	J 6
G	Green	P 11.3
G	Gulf	O 3

V Index of Abbreviations

Gp Fl	Group flashing	P 10.4
Gp Occ	Group occulting	P 10.2
h	Hard	J 39
h	Hour	B 49
H	Pilot transferred by helicopter	T 1.4
HAT	Highest astronomical tide	H 3
Hbr Mr	Harbormaster	F 60
Historic Wk	Historic wreck	N 26
Hk	Hulk	F 34
Hor	Horizontally disposed	P 15
Hor Cl	Horizontal clearance	D 21
Hosp	Hospital	F 62.2
hr	Hour	B 49
hrd	Hard	J 39
IALA	International Association of Lighthouse Authorities	Q 130
In	Inlet	O 10
Intens	Intensified	P 45
Int Qk Fl	Interrupted quick flashing	P 10.6
IQ	Interrupted quick flashing	P 10.6
I Qk Fl	Interrupted quick flashing	P 10.6
Iso	Isophase	P 10.3
IUQ	Interrupted ultra quick	P 10.8
km	Kilometer(s)	B 40
kn	Knot(s)	B 52
L	Loch, lough, lake	O 6
Lag	Lagoon	O 8
LANBY	Large Automatic Navigational Buoy	P 8
Lat, lat	Latitude	B 1
LASH	Lighter aboard ship	G 184
LAT	Lowest astronomical tide	H 2
Ldg	Landing	F 17
Ldg	Leading	P 21
Le	Ledge	O 28
L Fl	Long flashing	P 10.5
Lndg	Landing	F 17
LNG	Liquified natural gas	G 185
Long, long	Longitude	B 2
LOP	Line of position	S 21, S 31, S 41
LPG	Liquified petroleum gas	G 186
LSS	Life saving station	T 12
Lt	Light	P 1

Lt Ho	Lighthouse	P 1
Lt V	Light vessel	O 6
m	Meter(s)	B 41
m	Minute(s) of time	B 50
m	Medium (in relation to sand)	J 31
M	Mud, muddy	J 2
M	Nautical mile(s)	B 45
mag	Magnetic	B 61
MHHW	Mean higher high water	H 13
MHLW	Mean higher low water	H 14
MHW	Mean high water	H 5
MHWN	Mean high water neaps	H 11
MHWS	Mean high water springs	H 9
Mi	Nautical mile(s)	B 45
min	Minute of time	B 50
Mk	Mark	Q 101
MLHW	Mean lower high water	H 15
MLLW	Mean lower low water	H 12
MLW	Mean low water	H 4
MLWN	Mean low water neaps	H 10
MLWS	Mean low water springs	H 8
mm	Millimeter(s)	B 44
Mo	Morse	P 10.9
MON, Mon	Monument	B 24, E 24
MSL	Mean sea level	H 6
Mt	Mountain	O 32
Mth	Mouth	O 19
N	North, northern	B 9
N	Nun	Q 20
NE	Northeast	B 13
NM	Nautical mile(s)	B 45
N Mi	Nautical mile(s)	B 45
No	Number	N 12.2
Np	Neap tide	H 17
NW	Northwest	B 15
NWS SIG STA	Weather signal station	T 29
Obsc	Obscured	P 43
Obscd	Obscured	P 43
Obs spot	Observation spot	B 21
Obstn	Obstruction	K 40, K 41, K 42
Obstr	Obstruction	K 41
Oc	Occulting	P 10.2
Occ	Occulting	P 10.2

V Index of Abbreviations

Occas	Occasional	P 50
ODAS	Ocean Data Acquisition System	Q 58
Or	Orange	P 11.7
P	Pebbles	J 7
P	Pillar	Q 23
PA	Position approximate	B 7
Pass	Passage, pass	O 13
PD	Position doubtful	B 8
PLT STA	Pilot station	T 3
Pk	Peak	O 35
Post Off	Post office	F 63
Priv, priv	Private	P 65, Q 70
Prod. well	Production well	L 20
PROHIB	Prohibited	N 2.2, N 20, N 21
Pyl	Pylon	D 26
Q	Quick flashing	P 10.6
Qk Fl	Quick flashing	P 10.6
R	Coast radio station providing QTG services	S 15
R	Red	P 11.2
R	Rocky	J 9
Ra	Radar reference line	M 32
Ra (conspic)	Radar conspicuous object	S 5
Ra Antenna	Dish aerial	E 31
Racon	Radar transponder beacon	S 3
Radar Sc.	Radar scanner	E 30.3
Radar Tr.	Radar tower	E 30.2
Radome, Ra Dome	Radar dome	E 30.4
Ra Ref	Radar reflector	S 4
RBn	Circular radiobeacon	S 10
RC	Circular radiobeacon	S 10
Rd	Roads, roadstead	O 22
RD	Directional radiobeacon	S 11
RDF	Radio direction finding station	S 14
Ref.	Refuge	Q 124
Rep	Reported	I 3
Rf	Reef	O 26
RG	Radio direction finding station	S 14
Rk	Rock	J 9
Rky	Rocky	J 9
R Mast	Radio mast	E 28
Ro Ro	Roll on Roll off	F 50
R Sta	Coast radio station providing QTG services	S 15
R Tower	Radio tower	E 29
Ru	Ruins	D 8, F 33.1
RW	Rotating radiobeacon	S 12
S	Sand	J 1
S	South, southern	B 11
S	Spar, spindle	Q 24
s	Second of time	B 51
SALM	Single Anchor Leg Mooring	L 12
SBM	Single Buoy Mooring	L 16
Sc	Scanner	E 30.3
Sd	Sound	O 12
SD	Sounding doubtful	I 2
SE	Southeast	B 14
sec	Second of time	B 51
sf	Stiff	J 36
sft	Soft	J 35
Sh	Shells	J 12
Shl	Shoal	O 25
Si	Silt	J 4
so	Soft	J 35
Sp	Spring tide	H 16
SP	Spherical	Q 22
Sp.	Spire	E 10.3
Spipe	Standpipe	E 21
SPM	Single point mooring	L 12
SS	Signal station	T 20
st	Stones	J 5
stf	Stiff	J 36
stk	Sticky	J 34
Str	Strait	O 11
Subm	Submerged	O 93
Subm piles	Submerged piles	K 43.1
Subm ruins	Submerged ruins	F 33.2
sy	Sticky	J 34
SW	Southwest	B 16
T	True	B 63
t	Metric ton(s)	B 53
Tel	Telephone, telegraph	D 27
Temp, temp	Temporary	P 54
Tk	Tank	E 32
Tr, Tr., TR	Tower	E 10.2, E 20
TT	Tree tops	C 14
TV Mast	Television mast	E 28
TV Tower	Television tower	E 29

V *Index of Abbreviations*

Uncov	Uncovers	K 11
UQ	Ultra quick	P 10.8
v	Volcanic	J 37
var	Variation	B 60
Vert	Vertically disposed	P 15
Vert Cl	Vertical clearance	D 20
Vi	Violet	P 11.5
Vil	Village	D 4
VLCC	Very large crude carrier	G 187
vol	Volcanic	J 37
VQ	Very quick	P 10.7
V Qk Fl	Very quick flash	P 10.7
W	West, western	B 12
W	White	P 11.1
Wd	Weed	J 13.1
WGS	World Geodetic System	S 50
Whf	Wharf	F 13
WHIS, Whis	Whistle	R 15
Wk	Wreck	K 20-23, K 26-27, K 30
Y	Yellow	P 11.6

V *Index of Abbreviations*

Supplementary National Abbreviations:

Apt	Apartment	Es
B	Black	Qq
bk	Black	Jas
bl	Black	Jas
Blds	Boulders	Je
br	Brown	Jaz
bu	Blue	Jau
Cap	Capitol	Et
ch	Chocolate	Jba
Chec	Checkered	Qo
Ck	Chalk	Jf
Cn	Cinders	Jp
Co	Company	Eu
Co Hd	Coral head	Ji
COLREGS	Collision regulations	Na
Corp	Corporation	Ev
cps	Cycles per second	Bj
CRD	Columbia River Datum	Hj
c/s	Cycles per second	Bj
Ct Ho	Court house	Eo
dec	Decayed	Jan
deg	Degree(s)	Bn
Di	Diatoms	Jaa
Diag	Diagonal bands	Qp
Discol water	Discolored water	Ke
dk	Dark	Jbd
Explos Anch	Explosives anchorage	Qk
Facty	Factory	Ed
F Gp Fl	Fixed and group flashing	Pd
fl	Flood	Hq
fly	Flinty	Jao
Fr	Foraminifera	Jy
Fu	Fucus	Jaf
GAB, Gab	Gable	Ei
GCLWD	Gulf Coast Low Water Datum	Hk
Gl	Globigerina	Jz
glac	Glacial	Jap
gn	Green	Jav
Govt Ho	Government house	Em
Grd	Ground	Ja
Grs	Grass	Jv
gty	Gritty	Jam
GUN	Fog gun	Rd
gy	Gray	Jbb
HECP	Harbor entrance control point	Tb
HHW	Higher high water	Hb
HS	High school	Eg
ht	Height	Hp
HW	High water	Hq
HWF & C	High water full and change	Hh
Hz	Hertz	Bg
in	Inch	Bc
ins	Inches	Bc
Inst	Institute	En
ISLW	Indian springs low water	Hg
K	Kelp	Ju
kc	Kilocycle	Bk
kHz	Kilohertz	Bh
kn	Knot(s)	Ho
La	Lava	Jl
LLW	Lower low water	He
LOOK TR	Lookout tower	Tf
lrg	Large	Jai
lt	Light	Jbc
Ltd	Limited	Er
LW	Low water	Hc
LWD	Low water datum	Hd
LWF & C	Low water full and change	Hi
m²	Square meter(s)	Ba
m³	Cubic meter(s)	Bb
Ma	Mattes	Jag
Magz	Magazine	El
Mc	Megacycle(s)	Bl
Mds	Madrepores	Jj
MHz	Megahertz	Bi
Ml	Marl	Jc
Mn	Manganese	Jq
Mo	Morse code	Rf
Ms	Mussels	Js
MTL	Mean Tide Level	Hf

V Index of Abbreviations

Supplementary National Abbreviations:

NAUTO	Nautophone	Rc
or	Orange	Jax
Oys	Oysters	Jr
Oz	Ooze	Jb
Pav	Pavilion	Ep
Pm	Pumice	Jm
Po	Polyzoa	Jad
Pt	Pteropods	Jac
Quar	Quarantine	Fd
Qz	Quartz	Jg
Rd	Radiolaria	Jab
rd	Red	Jay
rt	Rotten	Jaj
Ry	Railway, railroad	Db
Sc	Scoriae	Jo
Sch	Schist	Jh
Sch	School	Ef
Sem	Semaphore	Tg
Sh	Shingle	Jd
S-LFl	Short-long flashing	Pb
sml	Small	Jah
Spg	Sponge	Jt
Spi	Spicules	Jx
spk	Speckled	Jal
Stg	Seatangle	Jw
St M	Statute mile(s)	Be
St Mi	Statute mile(s)	Be
Str	Stream	Hl
str	Streaky	Jak
SUB-BELL	Submarine fog bell	Ra
Subm crib	Submerged crib	Ki
SUB-OSC	Submarine oscillator	Rb
Sub vol	Submarine volcano	Kd
T	Telephone	Eq,Qt
T	Short ton(s)	Bm
T	Tufa	Jn
Tel	Telegraph	Qs
Tel off	Telegraph office	Ek
ten	Tenacious	Jaq

unev	Uneven	Jbf
Univ	University	Eh
us	Microsecond(s)	Bf
usec	Microsecond(s)	Bf
vard	Varied	Jbe
vel	Velocity	Hn
vi	Violet	Jat
Vol Ash	Volcanic ash	Jk
wh	White	Jar
WHIS	Whistle	Qc
yd	Yard	Bd
yds	Yards	Bd
yl	Yellow	Jaw

W International Abbreviations

B	Positions, Distances, Directions, Compass	
PA	Position approximate	B 7
PD	Position doubtful	B 8
N	North	B 9
E	East	B 10
S	South	B 11
W	West	B 12
NE	Northeast	B 13
SE	Southeast	B 14
NW	Northwest	B 15
SW	Southwest	B 16
km	Kilometer(s)	B 40
m	Meter(s)	B 41
dm	Decimeter(s)	B 42
cm	Centimeter(s)	B 43
mm	Millimeter(s)	B 44
M	Nautical mile(s), Sea mile(s)	B 45
ft	Foot/feet	B 47
h	Hour	B 49
m, min	Minute(s) of time	B 50
s, sec	Second(s) of time	B 51
kn	Knot(s)	B 52
t	Ton(s)	B 53
cd	Candela (new candela)	B 54

D	Cultural Features	
Ru	Ruin	D 8

F	Ports	
Lndg	Landing for boats	F 17
RoRo	Roll-on, Roll-off Ferry	F 50

I	Depths	
ED	Existence doubtful	I 1
SD	Sounding doubtful	I 2

K	Rocks, Wrecks, Obstructions	
Br	Breakers	K 17
Wk	Wreck	K 20
Obstn	Obstruction	K 40

L	Offshore Installations, Submarine Cables, Submarine Pipelines	
Fla	Flare stack	L 11
Prod Well	Submerged Production Well	L 20

M	Tracks, Routes	
Ra	Radar	M 31
DW	Deep Water	M 27.2

N	Areas, Limits	
No	Number	N 12.2
DW	Deep Water	N 12.4

O	Hydrographic Terms	
SMt	Seamount	O 33

W International Abbreviations

P — Lights

Lt	Light	P 1
F	Fixed	P 10.1
Oc	Occulting	P 10.2
Iso	Isophase	P 10.3
Fl	Flashing	P 10.4
LFl	Long-flashing	P 10.5
Q	Quick	P 10.6
IQ	Interrupted quick	P 10.6
VQ	Very quick	P 10.7
IVQ	Interrupted very quick	P 10.7
UQ	Ultra quick	P 10.8
IUQ	Interrupted ultra quick	P 10.8
Mo	Morse Code	P 10.9
W	white	P 11.1
R	red	P 11.2
G	green	P 11.3
Bu	blue	P 11.4
Vi	violet	P 11.5
Y	yellow/orange/Amber	P 11.6
Or	orange	P 11.7
Am	Amber	P 11.8
Ldg	Leading light	P 20.3
Dir	Direction light	P 30
occas	occasional	P 50
R Lts	Air obstruction lights	P 61.2
Fog Det Lt	Fog detector light	P 62
Aero	Aeronautical	P 60/61.1

Q — Buoys, Beacons

B	Black	Q 81
Mk	Mark	Q 101
IALA	International Association of Lighthouse Authorities	Q 130

R — Fog Signals

Explos	Explosive	R 10
Dia	Diaphone	R 11
Whis	Whistle	R 15

S — Radar, Radio, Electronic Position-Fixing Systems

Ra	Coast Radar Station	S 1
Racon	Radar transponder beacon	S 3
RC	Circular (non-directional) marine radiobeacon	S 10
RD	Directional radiobeacon	S 11
RW	Rotating-pattern radiobeacon	S 12
RG	Radio direction-finding stations	S 14
R	QTG service, Coast radio stations	S 15
Aero RC	Aeronautical radiobeacon	S 16
WGS	World Geodetic System	S 50

T — Services

H	Pilots transferred by helicopter	T 1.4
SS	Signal station	T 20
INT	international	T 21

X List of Descriptors

Abbreviations
- international W
- national V

Aerial E 30-31
Aero light P 60
Airfields D 17
- Topographic terms G 116-118
Air obstruction lights P 51
Anchorage areas N 12-13
Anchorages N 10-12, 14
Areas N
- General N 1-2

Beacons
- Colors Q 2-5
- General Q 80-83
- Position Q 1
- Topmarks Q 9-11

Beacon towers Q 110-111
Boat harbor U 1
Breakwater F 4
Bridges D 20-24, Dd-f
Buildings D 5-6, 8, Ea-b, Ed, Ef-v
- Topographic terms G 60-98
Buoyage System, IALA Q 130
Buoys Q
- Colors Q 2-5, Qo-q
- Seasonal Q 70-71
- Shapes Q 20-26
- Special purpose Q50-62 Qa-n,
- Topmarks Q 9-11

Cairn Q 100
Camping site U 30
Canals F 40-41
Caravan site U 29
Cargo transshipment area N 64
Car park U 27
Causeway F 3
Cemetery E 19
Chart number A 1-3
Chart title A 10
Chimney E 22
Churches E 10-12
Clearing line M 2
Coast
- Nature C 1-3, 5-9
- Topographic terms G 1-13
Coastguard T 10-11
Coastline C 1-9, Ca-e
Coast radar station S 1
Coast radio station S 15
Control Points B 20-24
Cranes F 53
Cultural Features D
Currents H 40-46, Hl-t
Cutting D 14

Dams F 44

Dates B49-51
Daytime light P 51
Decca lanes S 20-25
Deep water route M 27
Degaussing range N 25
Depths I
- General I 1-3
- in fairways and areas I 20-25, Ia-c
Depth contours I 30-31
Diffuser L 43

Direction lights P 30-31
Directions B 4-6, B 9-16
Dish aerial E 31
Docks F 25-27
Dolphin F 20-21
Dredging area N 63
Dumping grounds N 23-24, Nc-d
Dike F 1

Electronic Position Fixing Systems S 20-42
- Decca S 20-25
- Loran C S 30-37
- Omega S 40-42
Elevation (height) of light H20, P13
Embankment D 15
Explosives dumping ground N 23

Ferries M 50-51
Fish haven K 46
Flare stack
- on land E 23
- on sea L 11
Flood barrage F 43
Floodlight P 63
Fog detector light P 62
Fog light P 52
Fog signals R
- Descriptions R 20-22
- Types R 10-16, Ra
Forts E 34
Foul K 31-32
- explosives N 23
Fuel station U 18

Geographical positions B 1-16
Glacier C 25
Groin F 6
Harbor installations F 10-34, Fa-d
- Topographic terms G 170-187
Height of light H20, P13
Heights C 10-14, E 4-5
Historic wreck N 26
Hulk F 34
Hydraulic structures F 1-6
- Hydrographic terms O 67
- Topographic terms G 130-136
Hydrographic terms O
- Hydraulic structures O 67

X List of Descriptors

- Natural features O 1-9, 12, 15, 17-19, 23-66
- Nautical O 10-11, 13-14, 16, 20-22
- Notes O 80-94

IALA Buoyage System Q 130
Incineration area N 65
Inshore traffic zone M 25
International Abbreviations W
International boundaries N 40-41

Landmarks D 8, E
- General E 1-5
Lava Flow C 26
Layout of a chart, schematic A
Leading beacons Q 120
Leading lights P 20
Leading lines M 1
Levee F 1
Light characteristics P 10
Lighted marks Q 7-8
Lights floats Q 30-31
Lights
- Characteristics P 10
- Colors P 11
- Elevation P 13
- Disposition P 15
- Range P 14
- Structure P 1-8
- with limited times of exhibition P 50-55

Limits
- General N 1-2
- international N 40-41
- national N 42-47
- of ice N 60
- various N 48-49, 60-65, Na-b, Ne-f
Locks F 41-42
Log boom N 61
Loran C lanes S 30-37
Magnetic compass B 60-82
Marabout E 18
Marginal notes A
Marine farm K 48
Marina U 1
Mark Q 101
Masts E 27-28, E 30
Military area N 31
Military practice area N 30-34
Mills E 25, Ec
Mines E 35-36
Monument E 24
Mooring buoys Q 40-44, Qs-t
Mosque E 17
National limits N 48-49
Natural features C
- Hydrographic terms O 1-9, 12, 15, 17-18, 23-66
- Topographic terms G 20-39
Nature of the coast C 1-3, C 5-9
Nature of the seabed J

Nature reserve N 22
Notes
- Hydrographic terms O 80-94
Notice board Q 126

Obstructions K 40-47, K f-i
- General K 1-2
Oil barrier F 29
Offshore installations L
- General L 1-2
- Limits L 3-4
Omega lanes S 40-42
Overhead cable D 26-27 Dh
Overhead pipe D 28

Perch Q 91
Period P 12, P 50-55
Pile F 22, K 43
Pilotage T 1-4
Pipelines L 40-44
- areas L 40-41
- on land D 29
Platforms L 2, 10-14, 22
Pole Q 90
Ports F
- Topographic terms G 137-156
Positions B, B 30-33
- geographical B 1-16
Private light P 65
Prohibited area N 2
- Military N 31
Production platform L 10
Public buildings F 60-63

Quality of the bottom J, Jag-bf

Racon S 3-5
Radar S 1-5
- Surveillance System M 30-32
Radar beacon S 2
Radar reflector Q 10-11, S 4-5
Radar scanner E 30
Radar transponder beacon S 3
Radio S 10-16
Radiobeacon S 10-14, S 16
Radio Reporting Points M 40
Railways D 13, D 16, Db-c
- Topographic terms G 112
Ra mark S 2
Range P 14
Recommended route M 28
Recommended tracks M 3-6
Refuge beacon Q 124
Relief C 10-14, E 4-5, K 10, Cf-g
Rescue T 11-13
Restricted areas M 14, N 2, 20-26
Roads D 7, D 10-12, Da
- Topographic terms G 110-111, G 113-115
Rocks K 10-15 Ka

X List of Descriptors

- General   K 1-2
Routing measures   M 10-29
Routes   M
Ruins
- Harbor installations   F 33
- Landmarks   D 8

Salt pans   C 24
Satellite Navigation Systems   S 50
Schematic layout of a chart   A
Seawalls   F 2
Sector lights   P 40-46
Services   T
Settlements   D 1-4
- Topographic terms   G 50-54
Signal stations   T 20-31, T 33-36
Silo   E 33
Slip installations   F 23
Small craft facilities   U
Soundings   B 47-48, I 10-15
Special lights   P 60-65
Special purpose beacons   Q 120-126
Special purpose buoys   Q 50-62, Qa-n
Spoil ground   N 62
Strip light   P 64
Stake   K 44, Q 90-91
Submarine cables   L 30-32
- areas   L 30-31
Submarine pipelines   L 40-44
- areas   L 40-41
Symbolized positions   B 30-33

Tanks   E 32
Telepheric   D 25
Temple   E 13-16
Terms
- Hydrographic   O
- Topographic   G
Tidal levels, schematic data   H 20
Tidal current table   H 31
Tides   H
- Abbreviations   H 1-17, Ha-k
Tide tables   H 30-31
Times   B 49-51
Topmarks   Q 9-11
Topographic terms
- Airfields   G 116-118
- Coast   G 1-13
- Harbor installations   G 170-187
- Hydraulic structures   G 130-136
- Natural features   G 20-29
- Ports   G 137-156
- Railways   G 112
- Roads   G 110-111, G 113-115
- Settlements   G 50-54
Tower beacons   Q 110-111
Towers   E 20-21, E 10, E 29-30
Training walls   F 5
Transhipment facilities   F 50-53

- Offshore installations   L 16
Transit   M 2
Tracks   M 1-6
Types of seabed   J 1-15, Ja-ai
- intertidal areas   J 20-22

Underwater rock   K 13-17, Kb
- General   K 1-2
Units   B 40-54, Ba-n
Unwatched light   P 53

Vegetation   C 30-34, Ci-o

Water features   C 20-23
Water police   U 31
Wellheads   L 21, 23, La
Withy   Q 92
Works   F 30-32
Wrecks   K 20-31, Kc
- General   K 1-2

Yacht berths   U 1

IALA MARITIME BUOYAGE SYSTEM
LATERAL MARKS REGION A

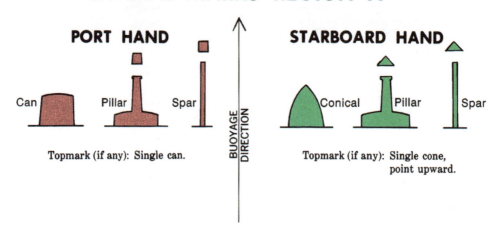

Lights, when fitted, may have any phase
characteristic other than that used
for preferred channels.

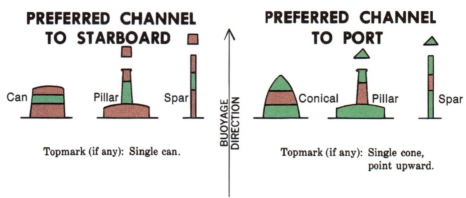

Lights, when fitted, are composite
group flashing Fl (2 + 1).

IALA MARITIME BUOYAGE SYSTEM
LATERAL MARKS REGION B

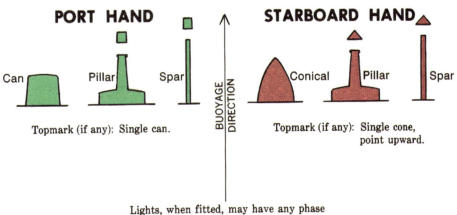

Lights, when fitted, may have any phase characteristic other than that used for preferred channels.

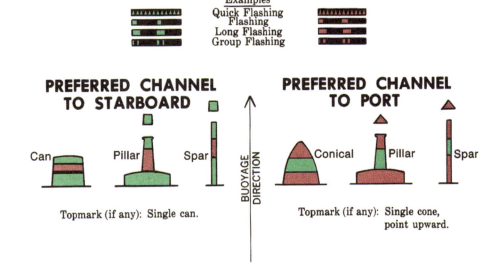

Lights, when fitted, are composite group flashing Fl (2+1).

IALA MARITIME BUOYAGE SYSTEM
CARDINAL MARKS REGIONS A AND B

Topmarks are always fitted (when practicable).
Buoy shapes are pillar or spar.

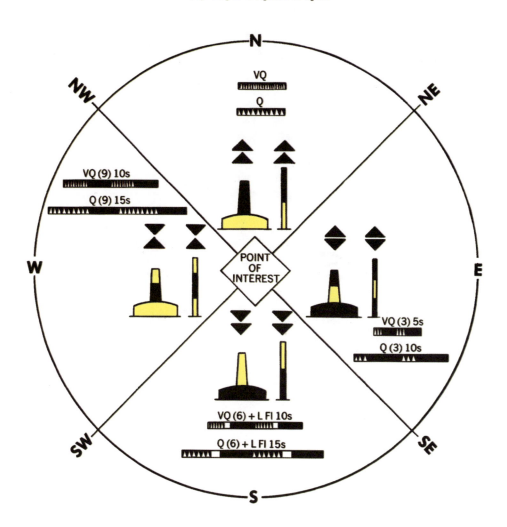

Lights, when fitted, are **white**. Very Quick Flashing
or Quick Flashing; a South mark also has a
Long Flash immediately following the quick flashes.

IALA MARITIME BUOYAGE SYSTEM
REGIONS A AND B

ISOLATED DANGER MARKS

Topmarks are always fitted (when practicable).

Shape: Optional, but not conflicting with lateral marks; pillar or spar preferred.

Light, when fitted, is **white**
Group Flashing (2)

Fl (2)

SAFE WATER MARKS

Topmark (if any): Single sphere.

Shape: Spherical or pillar or spar.

Light, when fitted, is **white**
Isophase or Occulting, or one Long Flash every 10 seconds or Morse "A"

Iso
Occ
L Fl 10s
Morse "A"

SPECIAL MARKS

Topmark (if any): Single X shape.

Shape: Optional, but not conflicting with navigational marks.

Light (when fitted) is **yellow** and may have any phase characteristic not used for white lights.

Examples
Fl Y
Fl(4) Y